cookingclass
cakes

step-by-step to the perfect cake

THE AUSTRALIAN
Women's Weekly

While you don't need a university degree to produce a perfect cake, patience, commonsense and attention to detail are all an advantage. Baking has long been one of my passions, so it's been a great pleasure to compile this book in the Cooking Class format. Armed with our insiders' knowledge, detailed step photography, and sections on tips, techniques and troubleshooting, you can be assured of faultless – and delicious – results every time.

Pamela Clark

Food Director

contents

tips and techniques

Baking a perfect cake may not be rocket science – but it does require a little background knowledge and a lot of attention to detail. The tips on the following pages will help set you straight.

oven types and rack position

There are many different types of ovens and energy sources, so it is important that you get to know your oven – particularly when it comes to baking cakes. The recipes in this book were tested in domestic-size electric ovens.

If using a fan-forced oven, check the operating instructions for best results. As a rule, reduce the baking temperature by 10°C to 20°C when using the fan during baking; cakes might also take slightly less time to bake than specified. Some ovens give better results if the fan is used for part of the baking time; it is usually best to introduce the fan about halfway through the baking time.

None of the recipes in this book has been tested in a microwave or microwave/convection oven, as the baking time and result would be different from a conventionally baked cake.

We positioned the oven racks and cake pan(s) so that the top of the baked cake will be roughly in the centre of the oven. If in doubt, check the manufacturer's instructions for your oven.

Several cakes can be baked at the same time, either on the same or different racks, provided they do not touch each other, or the oven wall or door, to allow for even circulation of heat.

To ensure even browning, cake pans on different racks should exchange positions about halfway through baking time; move the lower cakes to the top rack, and vice versa. This will not affect results if you do this carefully and quickly.

Best results are obtained by baking cakes in an oven preheated to the desired temperature; this takes about 10 minutes. This rule is particularly important for cakes which bake in under 30 minutes.

greasing pan with brush and melted butter

sprinkling flour over greased area

oven temperatures

These temperatures are only a guide. Always check the manufacturer's manual.

	°C (Celsius)	°F (Fahrenheit)	Gas Mark
Very slow	120	250	½
Slow	150	275-300	1-2
Moderately slow	160	325	3
Moderate	180	350-375	4-5
Moderately hot	200	400	6
Hot	220	425-450	7-8
Very hot	240	475	9

tracing around the base of pan   placing baking-paper collar in pan

how to prepare a cake pan

We used aluminium cake pans throughout this book because they give the best cake-baking results.

Cake pans made from materials having various coatings, such as non-stick, work well provided that the surface is unscratched. Pans made from tin and stainless steel do not conduct heat as evenly as does aluminium.

We found that oven temperatures should be lowered slightly (by about 10°C) when using cake pans other than those made of aluminium.

To grease a cake pan, use either a light, even coating of cooking-oil spray, or a pastry brush to brush melted butter or margarine evenly over the base and side(s).

Sometimes recipes call for a greased and floured cake pan. Simply grease the pan evenly (melted butter is best in this case)

and allow it to "set" a minute or two before sprinkling a little flour evenly over the greased area. Tap the pan several times on your bench then tip out the excess flour.

Cakes that are high in sugar, or that contain golden syrup, treacle or honey, have a tendency to stick so we recommend lining the base and/or side(s) of the pans. We have indicated in the recipes when this is necessary.

Trace around the base of the pan with a pencil onto greaseproof or baking paper; cut out the shape, slightly inside the pencil mark, so the paper fits snugly inside the greased pan. It is not necessary to grease the baking paper once it is in position.

As a guide, cakes requiring 1 hour or longer to bake should

have a baking paper "collar", extending about 5cm above the edge of the pan, to protect the top of the cake. The following method of lining round or square cake pans allows for this, using greaseproof or baking paper:

* For side(s), cut three paper strips long enough to fit around inside of the pan and 8cm wider than the depth of the pan. Fold strips lengthways about 2cm from the edge and make short diagonal cuts about 2cm apart, up to the fold (see photograph above). This helps ease the paper around the curves or corners of the pan, with cut section fitting around the base.

* Using base of pan as a guide, cut three paper circles (or squares) as instructed previously; position in base of pan after lining sides.

cake-making tips

- We do not recommend mixing cakes in blenders or processors unless specified in individual recipes.
- Use an electric beater to mix cakes, and always have the ingredients at room temperature, particularly the butter. Melted or extremely soft butter will alter the texture of the baked cake.
- Start mixing ingredients on a low speed; once mixture is combined, increase the speed to about medium and beat for the required time.
- Creamed mixtures for cakes can be mixed with a wooden spoon, but this takes longer.
- When measuring liquids, always stand the marked measuring jug on a flat surface and check at eye level for accuracy.
- Spoon measurements should be levelled off with a knife or spatula. Be careful when measuring ingredients such as honey or treacle.

to test if a cake is cooked

All cake baking times are approximate. Check your cake just after the suggested cooking time; it should be browned and starting to shrink from the side(s) of the pan. Feel the top with your fingertips; it should feel firm.

You may want to insert a thin skewer in the deepest part of the cake from top to base (we prefer to use a metal skewer rather than a wooden one because any mixture that adheres to it is easier to see). Gently remove the skewer; it shouldn't have any uncooked mixture clinging to it. Do not confuse cake mixture with stickiness from fruit.

cooling a cake

We have suggested standing cakes for up to 30 minutes before turning onto wire racks to cool further. The best way to do this, after standing time has elapsed,
is to hold the cake pan firmly and shake it gently, thus loosening the cake from the pan. Turn the cake, upside down, onto a wire rack, then turn the cake top-side up immediately using a second rack (unless directed otherwise). Some wire racks mark the cakes, particularly soft cakes such as sponges. To prevent this, cover the rack with baking paper.

We have indicated when it is best to cool cakes in pans; these are always covered with foil before cooling, and are mostly fruit cakes.

top: use a metal skewer to test if cake is cooked
bottom: turn the cake top-side up using a second wire rack

how to keep a cake

We have suggested maximum cake-keeping times at the end of each recipe. Most cakes keep well for 2 or 3 days depending on the climate and type of cake but, as a rule, remember that the higher the fat content, the longer the cake keeps.

■ Make sure your cake is at room temperature before storing it in an airtight container as close in size to the cake as possible; this minimises the amount of air around the cake.

■ For those cakes that are well suited to freezing, it is usually better to freeze them unfilled and un-iced because icing often cracks during the thawing process. Cakes thaw best overnight in the refrigerator. Wrap or seal cakes in freezer wrap or freezer bags, expelling as much air as possible.

■ We prefer to store rich fruit cakes in the refrigerator simply because they'll cut better; once sliced, they quickly return to room temperature.

faultless baking every time

Unfortunately, cakes don't always emerge from the oven looking just like our photographs. The following is a troubleshooters' guide to get you and your cake(s) back on track.

my butter cake wasn't perfect...

Sinks in centre while still baking If the mixture is forced to rise too quickly because the oven is too hot, it will sink in the centre.

Sinks in centre after removal from oven This generally means that the cake is undercooked.

Sugary crust Butter and sugar have not been creamed sufficiently.

White specks on top Undissolved sugar, or insufficient creaming. In a light butter cake, it is better to use caster sugar, which dissolves easily.

Excessive shrinking The oven being too hot has caused cake to overcook.

Rises and cracks in centre Cake pan too small or oven too hot. Most cakes baked in loaf, bar or ring pans crack slightly due to the confined space.

Crumbles when cut Mixture may have been creamed too much, or eggs added too quickly, causing curdling.

Sticks to pan Too much sugar or other sweetening in recipe. If a recipe contains honey or golden syrup, or if you're using a new pan, it is wise to line the evenly greased pan with greased baking paper.

Collar around top outside edge Cake baked at too high a temperature.

Pale on top, brown underneath and sides Too large a pan, or lining paper too high around sides of pan.

Colour streaks on top Insufficient mixing of ingredients, or bowl scrapings not mixed thoroughly into cake mixture in pan.

Uneven rising Oven shelf not straight, stove not level on floor, or mixture not spread evenly in pan.

Holes in baked cake Mixture not creamed sufficiently or oven too hot.

Crusty, overbrowned, uncooked in centre Cake baked too long or at too high a temperature. Cake pan too small, causing top to overcook while cake not cooked through completely.

my rich fruit cake wasn't perfect...

Fruit sinks to bottom Fruit washed but not dried thoroughly; cake mixture too soft to support weight of fruit (caused by over-creaming). Self-raising flour may have been used in recipe instead of plain flour. Fruit should be finely chopped so mixture can support it more easily.

Creamed mixture curdles Eggs and butter not at room temperature to begin with, or eggs not added quickly enough to creamed butter and sugar mixture, or eggs used are too large for mixture to absorb the excess liquid. If eggs used are larger than 60g in weight, omit one of the number shown in ingredients list, or add only the yolk of one of the eggs. Curdled creamed mixture could cause the finished cake to crumble when cut.

Doughy in centre Cake baked in too cold an oven, or not long enough.

Burnt bottom Wrong oven position. Cake baked at too high a temperature, or incorrect lining of pans. Rich fruit cakes require protection during long, slow baking time. Cakes which are 22cm or smaller require three thicknesses of baking-paper lining; larger cakes need one or two sheets of brown paper and three sheets of baking paper.

Cracks on top Cake baked at too high a temperature.

Sinks in middle Self-raising flour used, or too much bicarbonate of soda. (Usually only plain flour is used in rich fruit cake, but sometimes a small portion of self-raising flour is added). Cake may not have been baked properly. To test, push sharp-pointed knife through centre to base of pan; blade surface helps distinguish between uncooked mixture or fruit and cooked mixture. Test only after minimum specified baking time.

Crusty top Cake may have been baked at too high a temperature, on wrong shelf of oven, or too long. Cake should be baked in lower half of oven, at a slow temperature. If cake is 25cm or over, oven should be reduced to very slow after 1 hour of baking time. Lining paper should extend 5cm to 7cm above edge of pan; if it doesn't, the cake mixture will not be sufficiently protected during the long baking time. A crusty top will also occur if cake is not cooled correctly. When cake is removed from oven, brush top evenly with sherry, rum or brandy. Wrap cake, still in its pan, in aluminium foil to keep it airtight; this traps steam and helps keep top soft.

Colour streaks on top Insufficient mixing of ingredients, or bowl scrapings not mixed thoroughly into cake mixture in pan.

Uneven on top Oven shelf or stove not level, or mixture not spread evenly in pan (use a wet spatula to level top of cake mixture).

my sponge cake wasn't perfect...

Shrinks in oven Cake baked at too high a temperature or for too long.

Shrinks and wrinkles during cooling Insufficient baking time, or cooling the cake in a draught.

Small white specks on top Undissolved sugar; sugar should be added gradually to beaten eggs and beaten until completely dissolved between additions.

Flat and tough Incorrect folding in of the flour and liquid. Triple-sifted flour should be folded into mixture in a gentle, circular motion.

Pale and sticky on top Baking at too low an oven temperature, or wrong oven position.

Crusty Baking at too high an oven temperature, wrong oven position, or pan too small. Using high-sided cake pans protects the cake mixture.

Streaks on top Scrapings from mixing bowl not mixed into sponge mixture; scrapings are always slightly darker than the full amount of mixture.

Sinks in centre Pan too small, causing cake to rise quickly, then fall in the centre. Oven temperature may be too high, also causing sponge to rise too quickly. Sponge may be undercooked or oven door may have been opened during first half of baking.

measuring up

helpful measures

The difference between one country's measuring cups and another's is, at most, within a 2 or 3 teaspoon variance. (For the record, one Australian metric measuring cup holds approximately 250ml.) The most accurate way of measuring dry ingredients is to weigh them. When measuring liquids, use a clear glass or plastic jug with the metric markings. (One Australian metric tablespoon holds 20ml; one Australian metric teaspoon holds 5ml.)

If you would like to purchase *The Australian Women's Weekly* Test Kitchen's metric measuring cups and spoons (as approved by Standards Australia), turn to page 120 for details and order coupon. You will receive:

- a graduated set of four cups for measuring dry ingredients, with sizes marked on the cups.
- a graduated set of four spoons for measuring dry and liquid ingredients, with amounts marked on the spoons.

Note: North America, NZ and the UK use 15ml tablespoons. All cup and spoon measurements are level.

We use large eggs having an average weight of 60g.

how to measure

When using graduated metric measuring cups, shake dry ingredients loosely into the appropriate cup. Do not tap the cup on a bench or tightly pack the ingredients unless directed to do so. Level top of measuring cups and measuring spoons with a knife. When measuring liquids, place a clear glass or plastic jug with metric markings on a flat surface to check accuracy at eye level.

liquid measures

metric	imperial
30ml	1 fluid oz
60ml	2 fluid oz
100ml	3 fluid oz
125ml	4 fluid oz
150ml	5 fluid oz ($^1/_4$ pint/1 gill)
190ml	6 fluid oz
250ml	8 fluid oz
300ml	10 fluid oz ($^1/_2$ pint)
500ml	16 fluid oz
600ml	20 fluid oz (1 pint)
1000ml (1 litre)	1$^3/_4$ pints

level top of measuring cup with knife

dry measures

metric	imperial
15g	$^1/_2$oz
30g	1oz
60g	2oz
90g	3oz
125g	4oz ($^1/_4$lb)
155g	5oz
185g	6oz
220g	7oz
250g	8oz ($^1/_2$lb)
280g	9oz
315g	10oz
345g	11oz
375g	12oz ($^3/_4$lb)
410g	13oz
440g	14oz
470g	15oz
500g	16oz (1lb)
750g	24oz (1$^1/_2$lb)
1kg	32oz (2lb)

favourite cakes

cream-cheese lemon cake

PREPARATION TIME 15 MINUTES • BAKING TIME 1 HOUR

A rich, lemony-tasting cake, this keeps particularly well due to its high fat content. The eggs provide the only liquid in this recipe.

Adding last batch of flour to bowl

Spreading mixture into prepared pan

185g butter, softened
185g cream cheese, softened
**1 tablespoon finely grated
   lemon rind**
1¹/₂ cups (330g) caster sugar
3 eggs
1 cup (150g) self-raising flour
²/₃ cup (100g) plain flour

1 Position oven shelves; preheat oven to moderate. Grease 20cm baba pan.

2 Beat butter, cheese and rind together in small bowl with electric mixer until light in colour. Add sugar; beat until light and fluffy. Beat in eggs, one at a time, until just combined.

3 Add flours, in two batches; beat on low speed until just combined. Spoon mixture into prepared pan.

4 Bake cake in moderate oven about 1 hour. Turn cake onto wire rack to cool. Dust cake with a little sifted icing sugar, if desired.

SERVES 16

per serving 14.5g fat; 1105kJ

TIPS Mix the cake ingredients in a small bowl to work maximum volume into the mixture.

• Use the low speed on your electric mixer when you add each ingredient, then increase speed to about medium so that all ingredients are well incorporated and that mixture becomes smooth.

• Lemon rind can be substituted with another citrus rind, such as orange, lime or mandarin, or you can use 1 teaspoon of your favourite essence rather than the citrus rind.

• Cover cake loosely with foil about halfway during baking time if it starts to overbrown.

storage Cake will keep well in an airtight container for up to 1 week at room temperature or even longer in an airtight container in the refrigerator.

Cake can be frozen for up to 3 months.

TIPS For best results, use butter, milk and eggs that have reached room temperature. There is no need to sift the dry ingredients; however, if the bicarbonate of soda is lumpy, push it through a small sieve.

• Any essence can be substituted for vanilla; for a citrus flavour, add 2 teaspoons finely grated rind, such as orange, lemon or lime.

• To give this cake a slight caramel flavour, substitute $1^1/_3$ cups (275g) firmly packed brown sugar for the caster sugar.

storage This cake will keep in an airtight container for up to 3 days.

Cake can be frozen for up to 3 months.

cut 'n' keep butter cake

PREPARATION TIME 15 MINUTES • BAKING TIME 1 HOUR 15 MINUTES

This is an easy-to-mix, one-bowl, plain cake – and there's nothing nicer with a cuppa. Simply dust it with a little sifted icing sugar when serving.

125g butter, softened
1 teaspoon vanilla essence
1¼ cups (275g) caster sugar
3 eggs
1 cup (150g) plain flour
½ cup (75g) self-raising flour
¼ teaspoon bicarbonate of soda
½ cup (125ml) milk

1 Position oven shelves; preheat oven to moderately slow. Grease deep 20cm-round cake pan; line base with baking paper.

2 Beat ingredients in medium bowl on low speed with electric mixer until just combined.

3 Beat on medium speed until mixture is smooth and changed to a paler colour. Pour mixture into prepared pan.

4 Bake cake in moderately slow oven about 1¼ hours. Stand cake 5 minutes then turn onto wire rack; turn cake top-side up to cool. Dust cake with a little sifted icing sugar, if desired.

SERVES 22

per serving 5.7g fat; 581kJ

Mixing ingredients until just combined

Beating mixture until changed in colour

Pouring mixture into prepared pan

orange poppy seed syrup cake

PREPARATION TIME 25 MINUTES • BAKING TIME 1 HOUR

A popular combination of flavours makes this syrupy cake a safe bet to be loved by everybody. And, if you prefer to omit the syrup completely, the cake itself is still deliciously moist.

Finely grating orange rind, avoiding white pith

Adding poppy seed mixture to bowl

Pouring hot syrup over hot cake

1/3 cup (50g) poppy seeds
1/4 cup (60ml) milk
185g butter, softened
1 tablespoon finely grated orange rind
1 cup (220g) caster sugar
3 eggs
1 1/2 cups (225g) self-raising flour
1/2 cup (75g) plain flour
1/2 cup (60g) almond meal
1/2 cup (125ml) orange juice

ORANGE SYRUP
1 cup (220g) caster sugar
2/3 cup (160ml) orange juice
1/3 cup (80ml) water

1 Position oven shelves; preheat oven to moderate. Grease deep 22cm-round cake pan; line base and side with baking paper.

2 Combine seeds and milk in small bowl; stand 20 minutes.

3 Meanwhile, beat butter, rind and sugar in small bowl with electric mixer until light and fluffy; beat in eggs, one at a time, until just combined between additions.

4 Transfer mixture to large bowl; using wooden spoon, stir in flours, almond meal, juice and poppy seed mixture. Spread mixture into prepared pan.

5 Bake cake in moderate oven about 1 hour. Stand cake 5 minutes then turn onto wire rack over tray; turn top-side up, pour hot syrup over hot cake. Return any syrup that drips onto tray to jug; pour over cake.

orange syrup Using a wooden spoon, stir combined ingredients in small saucepan over heat, without boiling, until sugar dissolves; bring to a boil. Reduce heat; simmer, uncovered, without stirring, 2 minutes. Pour syrup into heatproof jug.

SERVES 16

per serving 14.3g fat; 1310kJ

TIPS If you don't particularly like citrus flavouring, substitute 1 teaspoon almond essence for the orange rind, and milk for the juice in the cake, and water for the juice in the orange syrup.

• Lemon or mandarin flavours also blend with the taste of poppy seeds; substitute, in equal amounts, for the orange rind and juice given above.

storage Cake with syrup can be kept in an airtight container for up to 2 days. Cake without syrup can be kept in an airtight container for up to 2 days, but can be frozen for up to 3 months.

Stirring in nuts, brandy and flours

Pouring hot lemon syrup over hot cake

brandied walnut cake with lemon syrup

PREPARATION TIME 20 MINUTES • BAKING TIME 1 HOUR

The walnuts, ground very finely, make up the majority of the "flour" content of this mixture.

2 cups (200g) walnuts, toasted
125g butter, softened
3 teaspoons finely grated
   lemon rind
²/3 cup (150g) caster sugar
1 egg
2 tablespoons brandy
¹/3 cup (50g) plain flour
¹/3 cup (50g) self-raising flour

LEMON SYRUP
¹/4 cup (60ml) lemon juice
¹/4 cup (55g) caster sugar

1 Position oven shelves; preheat oven to moderately slow. Grease deep 20cm-round cake pan; line base with baking paper.

2 Blend or process nuts until finely ground.

3 Beat butter, rind, sugar and egg in small bowl with electric mixer until light and fluffy. Transfer mixture to large bowl; using wooden spoon, stir in brandy, nuts and flours. Spread mixture into prepared pan.

4 Bake cake in moderately slow oven about 1 hour.

5 Pour hot lemon syrup over hot cake in pan. Cover pan tightly with foil; cool cake to room temperature.

lemon syrup Combine ingredients in small saucepan. Using wooden spoon, stir over heat, without boiling, until sugar dissolves; bring to a boil, remove from heat.

SERVES 12

per serving 20.6g fat; 1247kJ

TIPS Any kind of nut can be substituted for the walnuts. Buy exactly the same weight of either ready-ground nut meal or of nut pieces that you blend or process yourself. Pecans and orange, instead of lemon, is another good combination.

• Rum is a good substitute for the brandy, or you can use fruit juice if you don't want to use alcohol.

• Serve this cake warm, or at room temperature, with a little yogurt.

storage Cake with syrup can be kept in an airtight container for up to 2 days.

Cake without syrup can be kept in an airtight container for up to 2 days, and can be frozen for up to 3 months.

boiled date cake

PREPARATION TIME 20 MINUTES • BAKING TIME 40 MINUTES

This easy cake, made in a single saucepan, can be served warm with cream, custard or ice-cream, cold with butter, or just on its own.

Chopping dates roughly with scissors

Adding soda to date mixture

Spooning mixture into the well-greased pan

185g butter, chopped
1 cup (250ml) milk
3/4 cup (150g) firmly packed
    brown sugar
1 cup (145g) coarsely chopped
    seeded dried dates
1/2 teaspoon bicarbonate of soda
11/2 cups (225g) self-raising flour
1/2 cup (75g) plain flour
2 eggs, beaten lightly

1 Position oven shelves; preheat oven to moderate. Grease a 20cm baba pan well.

2 Combine butter, milk, sugar and dates in large saucepan. Using wooden poon, stir over heat until butter melts. Bring to a boil; remove from heat, stir in soda. Stand 10 minutes.

3 Quickly stir in flours and egg. Spoon mixture into prepared pan.

4 Bake cake in moderate oven about 40 minutes. Turn cake onto wire rack to cool.

SERVES 16

per serving
11g fat; 949kJ

TIPS Seeded prunes can be substituted for dates. Chopping both prunes and dates is made easier by using kitchen scissors instead of a knife.

• The bicarbonate of soda not only helps soften the fruit, but also gives the cake a beautiful golden colour.

• It's important to grease the baba pan well; sugary mixtures such as this tend to stick to the pan.

• This cake can also be baked in a deep 20cm-round cake pan. Grease the pan and line the base. Bake in moderate oven about 55 minutes.

storage Cake will keep in an airtight container for up to 4 days at room temperature or up to 1 week in an airtight container in the refrigerator.

Cake can be frozen for up to 3 months.

almond butter cake

PREPARATION TIME 20 MINUTES • BAKING TIME 1 HOUR

A yummy, buttery cake best indulged in by grown-ups, as most children don't like the almond flavour.

375g butter, softened
1 teaspoon almond essence
1¹/₂ cups (330g) caster sugar
6 eggs
³/₄ cup (110g) self-raising flour
1¹/₂ cups (225g) plain flour
¹/₂ cup (60g) almond meal

Beating butter, essence and sugar thoroughly

Beating eggs into butter mixture

Folding in the dry ingredients

Spreading mixture into prepared pan

1 Position oven shelves; preheat oven to moderate. Grease deep 23cm-square cake pan; line base with baking paper.

2 Beat butter, essence and sugar in large bowl with electric mixer until light and fluffy; beat in eggs, one at a time, until combined between additions.

3 Using wooden spoon, stir in flours and almond meal, in two batches. Spread mixture into prepared pan.

4 Bake cake in moderate oven about 1 hour. Stand cake 5 minutes then turn onto wire rack; turn top-side up to cool. Dust cake with a little sifted icing sugar, if desired.

SERVES 16

per serving 23.5g fat; 1557kJ

21

TIPS Try substituting hazelnut meal for the almonds, and use vanilla instead of almond essence.

• This is one of those cakes that must be aerated well to achieve its light, ethereal texture, so be certain to beat the butter, essence, sugar and eggs well.

storage Cake will keep well in an airtight container for up to 3 days at room temperature or up to 1 week in an airtight container in the refrigerator.

Cake can be frozen for up to 3 months.

cinnamon teacake

PREPARATION TIME 15 MINUTES • BAKING TIME 30 MINUTES

Taking care to thoroughly beat the butter, essence, sugar and egg will result in a light-as-air texture to this cake, best when eaten warm with butter.

60g butter, softened
1 teaspoon vanilla essence
²/₃ cup (150g) caster sugar
1 egg
1 cup (150g) self-raising flour
¹/₃ cup (80ml) milk
10g butter, melted, extra
1 teaspoon ground cinnamon
1 tablespoon caster sugar, extra

1 Position oven shelves; preheat oven to moderate. Grease deep 20cm-round cake pan; line base with baking paper.

2 Beat butter, essence, sugar and egg in small bowl with electric mixer until very light and fluffy; this process will take between 5 and 10 minutes, depending on the type of mixer used.

3 Using wooden spoon, gently stir in sifted flour and milk. Spread mixture into prepared pan.

4 Bake cake in moderate oven about 30 minutes. Turn cake onto wire rack then turn top-side up; brush top with extra butter, sprinkle with combined cinnamon and extra sugar. Serve warm with butter, if desired.

SERVES 10

per serving 6.8g fat; 720kJ

Beating mixture until very light and fluffy

Spreading mixture into prepared pan

Sprinkling cinnamon and sugar over hot cake

TIPS The beauty of this cake is its lightness; most of the time in baking it is not necessary to sift flour, but this cake benefits from aeration, and sifting the flour will help lighten the mixture.

• To change the cake's flavour, omit the vanilla and substitute the essence of your choice, or beat in 2 teaspoons finely grated citrus rind (orange, lemon, lime, mandarin, etc) with the butter mixture.

• Melt the extra butter in a microwave oven on HIGH (100%) for 10 seconds.

storage This cake should be eaten immediately it is made.

jam roll

PREPARATION TIME 20 MINUTES • BAKING TIME 8 MINUTES

Also known as a jelly roll in the United States, this filled and rolled sponge cake has long been a favourite in Britain, although its true origins are obscure. Quick and easy to make yet very impressive-looking, slices of the roll are good served warm or at room temperature with a dollop of whipped cream.

3 eggs, separated
1/2 cup (110g) caster sugar
3/4 cup (110g) self-raising flour
2 tablespoons hot milk
1/4 cup (110g) caster sugar, extra
1/2 cup (160g) jam, warmed

1 Position oven shelves; preheat oven to moderately hot. Grease 25cm x 30cm swiss roll pan; line base and short sides of pan with a strip of baking paper, bringing paper 5cm over edges, grease paper.

2 Beat egg whites in small bowl with electric mixer until soft peaks form; gradually add sugar, 1 tablespoon at a time, beating until dissolved between additions.

3 With motor operating, add egg yolks, one at a time, beating until mixture is pale and thick; this will take about 10 minutes.

4 Meanwhile, sift flour three times onto baking paper.

5 Pour hot milk down side of bowl; add triple-sifted flour. Working quickly, use plastic spatula to fold milk and flour through egg mixture. Pour mixture into prepared pan, gently spreading mixture evenly into corners.

6 Bake cake in moderately hot oven about 8 minutes or until top of cake feels soft and springy when touched lightly with fingertips.

7 Meanwhile, place a piece of baking paper cut the same size as cake on board or bench; sprinkle evenly with extra sugar. When cooked, immediately turn cake onto sugared paper, quickly peeling away the lining paper. Working rapidly, use serrated knife to cut away crisp edges from all sides of cake.

8 Using hands, gently roll cake loosely from one of the short sides; unroll, spread evenly with jam.

9 Roll cake again, from same short side, by lifting paper and using it to guide the roll into shape.

10 Either serve jam roll immediately with cream, or place onto wire rack to cool.

SERVES 10

per serving 1.9g fat; 711kJ

Beating egg whites until soft peaks form

Folding in flour and milk

Trimming all sides of sponge

Rolling jam roll, using paper as guide

TIPS While this is easy to make, it may take a bit of experimentation with your oven to determine the best temperature and to perfect the timing – two elements that are critical for the success of this sponge cake. Every oven is slightly different to another; be guided by the manufacturer's instructions for your oven. As a guide, the second shelf up from the oven floor is usually the best position for the cake pan and the temperature should be 200°C in a fan-forced oven.

• Gentle folding of the milk and flour through the egg mixture is also important for success; heavy handling of the mixture equals a heavy sponge cake. Use whatever kitchen tool you feel most comfortable with to incorporate the ingredients. Some people prefer to use a large metal spoon, some their hand or a rubber or plastic spatula; it doesn't matter what you use, it's how you use it that's important.

• Jam can be warmed for about 20 seconds in a microwave oven on HIGH (100%).

storage Cake must be made the day it is served.

Peeling beetroot with vegetable peeler

Coarsely grating beetroot

Stirring ingredients together

Spreading mixture into prepared pan

beetroot cake

PREPARATION TIME 25 MINUTES • BAKING TIME 1 HOUR 30 MINUTES

Moist, and fresh- and earthy-tasting, this cake owes all of its finer points to the inclusion of the beetroot.

3 small fresh beetroot (250g), trimmed
250g butter, softened
3 teaspoons finely grated lemon rind
1 cup (220g) caster sugar
4 eggs
1 cup (150g) dried currants
1 cup (150g) plain flour
1 cup (150g) self-raising flour

1 Position oven shelves; preheat oven to moderate. Grease deep 20cm-round cake pan; line base and side with baking paper.

2 Using a vegetable peeler, peel beetroot thinly; coarsely grate beetroot.

3 Beat butter, rind and sugar in small bowl with electric mixer until light and fluffy. Beat in eggs, one at a time, beating until just combined between additions. Mixture might curdle at this stage, but will come together later.

4 Transfer butter mixture to large bowl. Using wooden spoon, stir in beetroot, currants and flours. Spread mixture into prepared pan.

5 Bake cake in moderate oven about 1½ hours.

6 Stand cake 10 minutes, then turn onto wire rack; turn top-side up to cool. Dust with sifted icing sugar, if desired.

SERVES 22

per serving 10.5g fat; 852kJ

TIPS It's a good idea to wear disposable gloves when peeling and grating beetroot, as it will stain your skin. If you're using a wooden chopping board, wash it as fast as possible after beetroot has come into contact with it to remove stains. Scrubbing the board with coarse cooking salt should help remove any stubborn stains.

• The same amount of coarsely grated carrot or zucchini can be substituted for beetroot.

• Sultanas, chopped raisins, or finely chopped seeded dates could be substituted for currants.

storage Cake can be kept in an airtight container for up to 1 week, or in refrigerator for up to 3 weeks.

Cake can be frozen for up to 3 months.

polenta fig cake

PREPARATION TIME 20 MINUTES • BAKING TIME 1 HOUR 30 MINUTES

Polenta is a flour-like substance made of ground corn (maize); it is slightly finer and lighter in colour than ordinary cornmeal.

1 cup (250g) caster sugar
1 cup (200g) polenta
1³/4 cups (430ml) milk
125g butter, softened
1 tablespoon finely grated orange rind
¹/2 cup (125g) caster sugar, extra
2 eggs
1 cup (150g) self-raising flour
¹/2 cup (75g) plain flour
1¹/2 cups (250g) coarsely chopped dried figs

Stirring milk into polenta and sugar

Spreading polenta mixture onto tray

Combining ingredients in bowl

1 Position oven shelves; preheat oven to moderately slow. Grease deep 20cm-round cake pan; line base with baking paper.

2 Place sugar and polenta in medium saucepan, using a wooden spoon, gradually stir in milk. Bring to a boil while stirring; reduce heat, simmer, stirring, about 4 minutes or until polenta is soft and thick. Spread polenta mixture onto greased tray; cool to room temperature.

3 Beat butter, rind and extra sugar in small bowl with electric mixer until light and fluffy; beat in eggs, one at a time, until just combined between additions.

4 Transfer mixture to large bowl, stir in polenta mixture, flours and figs. Spread mixture into prepared pan.

5 Bake cake in moderately slow oven 45 minutes; cover loosely with foil, bake about 45 minutes

6 Stand cake in pan 10 minutes, turn onto wire rack then turn top-side up to cool. Dust cake with a little sifted icing sugar, if desired.

SERVES 22

per serving 6.3g fat; 878kJ

TIPS Polenta mixture must be stirred constantly while cooking, to ensure a smooth mixture. It will take about 1 hour to cool.

• Finely chopped seeded dried dates could be substituted for figs. Lemon rind can be substituted for orange rind.

• Try this cake served with a dollop of cream or yogurt.

storage Cake can be kept at room temperature in an airtight container for up to 3 days.

whole-orange cake with macaroon topping

PREPARATION TIME 30 MINUTES • BAKING TIME 1 HOUR 30 MINUTES

Very moist and dense, this dessert cake has its origins in the citrus cakes of the eastern Mediterranean. Do not peel the oranges called for in this recipe.

2 medium oranges (480g)
5 eggs
1½ cups (175g) almond meal
1 cup (220g) caster sugar
½ cup (75g) self-raising flour
3 egg whites
¼ cup (55g) caster sugar, extra
¾ cup (65g) desiccated coconut

1 Place unpeeled oranges in medium saucepan, cover with cold water; bring to a boil, drain. Repeat process two more times then cool oranges to room temperature.

2 Position oven shelves; preheat oven to moderately hot. Grease 24cm springform pan; line base with baking paper.

3 Halve oranges; remove and discard seeds. Blend or process orange halves until pulpy; place in large bowl.

4 Using wooden spoon, beat eggs, almond meal, sugar and flour into orange mixture. Pour mixture into prepared pan.

5 Bake cake in moderately hot oven 1 hour.

6 Meanwhile, beat egg whites in small bowl with electric mixer until soft peaks form; with motor operating, gradually add extra sugar, beating until dissolved. Using fork, stir coconut into egg mixture. Remove cake carefully from oven, closing oven door to maintain temperature. Using metal spatula, spread coconut mixture evenly over cake; bake about 10 minutes or until topping is lightly browned.

7 Cool cake to room temperature before removing from pan.

SERVES 12

per serving 13.9g fat; 1162kJ

Removing seeds from cooked orange halves

Transferring pulped oranges to large bowl

Pouring mixture into prepared pan

TIPS It's best to bake this cake in a springform pan to make removal easy.

• You can substitute the same weight of mandarins for the oranges.

storage Cake will keep for up to 2 days in an airtight container in the refrigerator.

Spreading macaroon topping over cake

cafe cakes

mango coconut cake

PREPARATION TIME 35 MINUTES • BAKING TIME 1 HOUR 15 MINUTES

250g butter, softened
1 teaspoon coconut essence
1¹/2 cups (330g) caster sugar
4 eggs
²/3 cup (160ml) mango puree
2 cups (180g) desiccated coconut
2¹/2 cups (375g) self-raising flour

COCONUT FROSTING
1 egg white
1¹/4 cups (200g) icing
    sugar mixture
2 teaspoons mango puree
³/4 cup (65g) desiccated coconut

Combining ingredients in bowl

Beating egg white until foamy for frosting

1 Position oven shelves; preheat oven to moderate. Grease deep 22cm-round cake pan; line base with baking paper.

2 Beat butter, essence and sugar in small bowl with electric mixer until combined. Add eggs, one at a time, beating only until combined between additions.

3 Transfer mixture to large bowl. Using wooden spoon, stir in puree and coconut, then flour. Spread mixture into prepared pan.

4 Bake cake in moderate oven about 1¹/4 hours. Stand cake 5 minutes then turn onto wire rack; turn cake top-side up to cool.

5 Spread top of cold cake with coconut frosting.

coconut frosting Beat egg white in small bowl with electric mixer or rotary beater until foamy. Gradually beat in icing sugar, 1 tablespoon at a time; using fork, mix in puree and coconut. Cover frosting with plastic wrap until required, pressing plastic directly onto surface.

SERVES 12

per serving 32.5g fat; 2464kJ

TIPS Two teaspoons of finely grated lime rind can be used as a flavouring instead of (or as well as) the coconut essence.

• Because of this cake's high fat content, it is important the butter, sugar and egg mixture not be over-creamed.

• Peach or apricot nectar can be substituted for mango puree.

• You can buy frozen pureed mango at most supermarkets, or you can puree the flesh of a fresh mango (you need a mango weighing about 450g). Mango nectar can be substituted but the flavour will not be as intense.

• Cover cake loosely with foil during baking if it starts to overbrown.

• The surface of the frosting must be covered completely with plastic wrap to prevent air being trapped between the surface and covering; otherwise, a crust will develop, making the frosting more difficult to spread on the cake.

storage Cake will keep for up to 2 days in an airtight container.

Unfrosted cake can be frozen for up to 3 months.

lumberjack cake

PREPARATION TIME 30 MINUTES • BAKING TIME 1 HOUR 10 MINUTES

While the country of origin of this cake is somewhat in doubt (is it Australia or Canada?), the delicious taste has never been questioned.

2 large apples (400g), peeled, cored, chopped finely
1 cup (200g) finely chopped seeded dried dates
1 teaspoon bicarbonate of soda
1 cup (250ml) boiling water
125g butter, softened
1 teaspoon vanilla essence
1 cup (220g) caster sugar
1 egg
1¹/₂ cups (225g) plain flour

TOPPING
60g butter
¹/₂ cup (100g) firmly packed brown sugar
¹/₂ cup (125ml) milk
²/₃ cup (50g) shredded coconut

1 Position oven shelves; preheat oven to moderate. Grease deep 23cm-square cake pan; line base and sides with baking paper.

2 Combine apple, dates and soda in large bowl, add the water, cover bowl with plastic wrap; stand 10 minutes.

3 Meanwhile, beat butter, essence, sugar and egg in small bowl with electric mixer until light and fluffy.

4 Add creamed butter mixture to apple mixture; using wooden spoon, stir in flour well. Pour mixture into prepared pan.

5 Bake cake in moderate oven 50 minutes.

6 Remove cake carefully from oven to bench; close oven door to maintain correct oven temperature. Using metal spatula, carefully spread warm topping evenly over cake; return cake to oven, bake about 20 minutes or until topping has browned.

7 Stand cake 5 minutes then turn onto wire rack; turn cake top-side up to cool.

topping Combine ingredients in medium saucepan; using wooden spoon, stir topping mixture over low heat until butter melts and sugar dissolves.

SERVES 12

per serving 16.5g fat; 1569kJ

Finely chopping peeled and cored apples

Pouring water over apple, dates and soda

Spreading topping over partially baked cake

TIPS We used Granny Smith apples in this recipe, but any type of apple works just as well.

• Standing the apple mixture for 10 minutes allows the bicarbonate of soda to start softening the dates.

• Begin preparing the topping while cake is in oven for the first 50 minutes.

• The topping can be prepared in a microwave oven. Combine all ingredients in a medium microwave-safe bowl; cook, uncovered, on HIGH (100%) for about 1 minute or until butter melts and sugar dissolves.

storage Cake can be kept up to 1 week in an airtight container in the refrigerator.

Cake can be frozen for up to 3 months.

apple pecan cake with maple frosting

PREPARATION TIME 30 MINUTES • BAKING TIME 50 MINUTES

The wonderful combination of nuts and fruit with maple-flavoured syrup makes this delectably moist cake exceedingly more-ish.

90g butter, softened
1/2 cup (80g) wholemeal
    self-raising flour
1 cup (150g) white
    self-raising flour
1 teaspoon ground cinnamon
3/4 cup (150g) firmly packed
    brown sugar
1/4 cup (60ml) maple-
    flavoured syrup
3 eggs
1 cup (125g) coarsely
    chopped pecans
1/2 cup (85g) coarsely
    chopped raisins
1 cup (170g) coarsely
    grated apple
1/2 cup (60g) pecans, toasted, extra

MAPLE FROSTING
90g butter, softened
1 cup (160g) icing sugar mixture
1 teaspoon maple-flavoured syrup

1 Position oven shelves; preheat oven to moderate. Grease 20cm ring pan; line base and sides with baking paper.

2 Beat butter, flours, cinnamon, sugar, syrup and eggs in medium bowl on low speed with electric mixer until ingredients are combined. Beat on medium speed until mixture is smooth and changed in colour.

3 Using wooden spoon, stir in nuts, raisins and apple. Spoon mixture into prepared pan; spread evenly with plastic spatula.

4 Bake cake in moderate oven about 50 minutes. Stand cake 5 minutes then turn onto wire rack; turn cake top-side up to cool.

5 Spread cold cake with maple frosting; top with extra nuts.

maple frosting Beat ingredients in small bowl with electric mixer until light and fluffy.

SERVES 12

per serving 21.5g fat; 1715kJ

TIPS Sultanas or finely chopped seeded dates or prunes can be substituted for the raisins, and walnuts for the pecans.

• You need 1 large apple (200g) for this cake; we used the Granny Smith variety but any type of apple works equally well.

• This cake can be baked in two 8cm x 25cm bar cake pans. Bake in moderate oven for about 45 minutes.

storage Cake will keep for up to 3 days in an airtight container in the refrigerator.

Frosted or unfrosted, the cake can be frozen for up to 3 months.

Coarsely grating peeled apple

Beating butter mixture until smooth

Beating maple frosting ingredients together

sacher torte

PREPARATION TIME 40 MINUTES (plus standing time) • BAKING TIME 1 HOUR 10 MINUTES

This famous Viennese cake was originally made in 1832 by the grandfather of Eduard Sacher, founder of the Hotel Sacher, for the court of the Empire's Prince Metternich. The secret recipe was handed down to Eduard, who is responsible for popularising it on the hotel's menu... and on the menu of restaurants and cafes throughout the world.

100g dark chocolate, chopped coarsely
1 cup (250ml) water
125g butter, softened
1¼ cups (250g) firmly packed brown sugar
3 eggs
1 cup (150g) self-raising flour
¼ cup (25g) cocoa powder
½ cup (60g) almond meal
⅓ cup (110g) apricot jam, warmed, strained
50g dark chocolate, melted

GANACHE
200g dark chocolate, chopped coarsely
⅔ cup (160ml) cream

1 Position oven shelves; preheat oven to moderately slow. Grease deep 22cm-round cake pan, line base with baking paper.

2 Combine chopped chocolate and the water in small saucepan; using wooden spoon, stir over low heat until chocolate melts. Remove from heat.

3 Beat butter and sugar in small bowl with electric mixer until combined; beat in eggs, one at a time, only until combined. Mixture will curdle at this stage but will come together later.

4 Transfer mixture to large bowl; using wooden spoon, stir in sifted flour, cocoa, almond meal and warm chocolate mixture. Mix well, pour into prepared pan.

5 Bake cake in moderately slow oven about 1 hour and 10 minutes. Stand cake 10 minutes then turn onto wire rack; turn cake top-side up to cool.

6 Using serrated knife, split cold cake in half; sandwich layers with jam. Place cake on wire rack over tray; using metal spatula, spread a thin layer of ganache over cake.

7 Heat remaining ganache over saucepan of simmering water, stirring, until of pouring consistency; strain into medium jug. Using metal spatula and working quickly, pour ganache over cake, smoothing it all over top and side. Stand at room temperature until ganache sets.

8 Spoon melted chocolate into small paper piping bag; pipe SACHER on top of cake, allow to set at room temperature.

ganache Place chocolate and cream in small heatproof bowl; using wooden spoon, stir over small saucepan of simmering water until chocolate melts.

SERVES 12

per serving 27.7g fat; 1980kJ

Spreading cake with thin layer of ganache

Straining heated ganache into jug

TIPS Jam can be warmed in the microwave oven for about 10 seconds on HIGH (100%).

• When melting chocolate in a bowl set over simmering water in a pan on top of the stove, it is important that the water never touches the bottom of the bowl. The bowl should be of such a size that it sits comfortably over a saucepan of complementary size.

• Ganache sets at room temperature; if refrigerated, ganache will sweat.

storage Iced cake can be kept up to 3 days in an airtight container in the refrigerator. Uniced cake can be kept up to 1 week in an airtight container in the refrigerator.

Uniced cake can be frozen for up to 3 months.

TIPS Bruising cardamom pods helps release the flavour into the syrup.

• When grating or peeling citrus rind, avoid the bitter white pith.

• Instead of a knife, use your citrus zester to finely shred rind.

• Any syrup that drips onto the tray should be poured back over the cake.

• Lime, mandarin or orange juice and rind can be substituted for lemon.

• Wedges of cake can be warmed for about 30 seconds on HIGH (100%) in the microwave oven.

• You can bake this cake in a deep 20cm-round cake pan which has been greased, and the base of which has been lined with baking paper. Bake in a moderate oven for 1 hour 10 minutes.

storage Cake will keep for up to 4 days in an airtight container in the refrigerator.

yogurt and lemon syrup cake

PREPARATION TIME 25 MINUTES • BAKING TIME 50 MINUTES

This cake is sublime served warm with thick, fresh cream.

250g butter, softened
3 teaspoons finely grated
** lemon rind**
1 cup (220g) caster sugar
3 eggs
1/2 cup (45g) desiccated coconut
1/4 cup (30g) almond meal
2 tablespoons lemon juice
21/2 cups (375g)
** self-raising flour**
3/4 cup (200g) yogurt
1 medium lemon (140g)
1/2 cup (125ml) water
1/4 cup (90g) honey
4 cardamom pods, bruised

1 Position oven shelves; preheat oven to moderate. Grease 20cm baba pan.

2 Beat butter, rind and sugar in small bowl with electric mixer until light and fluffy. Add eggs, one at a time, beating well between additions.

3 Transfer mixture to large bowl; using wooden spoon stir in coconut, almond meal and juice, then flour and yogurt. Spoon mixture into prepared pan; spread evenly with plastic spatula.

4 Bake cake in moderate oven about 50 minutes. Stand cake 5 minutes then turn onto wire rack over tray.

5 Meanwhile, using vegetable peeler, remove rind from lemon; slice rind finely. Squeeze juice from lemon; you need 1/4 cup (60ml) juice.

6 Combine rind, juice, the water, honey and cardamom in small saucepan; stir over heat, without boiling, until honey melts. Bring to a boil; reduce heat then simmer, uncovered, 5 minutes. Using slotted spoon, carefully remove and discard cardamom.

7 Pour hot syrup over hot cake.

SERVES 12

per serving 23.2g fat; 1763kJ

Bruising cardamom pods with flat side of knife

Finely shredding lemon rind

Pouring hot syrup over hot cake

hummingbird cake

PREPARATION TIME 35 MINUTES • BAKING TIME 40 MINUTES

This moist, luscious cake from the American Deep South translates as delicious in anyone's language. You need approximately 2 large overripe (460g) bananas for this recipe.

450g can crushed pineapple in syrup
1 cup (150g) plain flour
1/2 cup (75g) self-raising flour
1/2 teaspoon bicarbonate of soda
1/2 teaspoon ground cinnamon
1/2 teaspoon ground ginger
1 cup (200g) firmly packed
  brown sugar
1/2 cup (45g) desiccated coconut
1 cup mashed banana
2 eggs, beaten lightly
3/4 cup (180ml) vegetable oil

CREAM CHEESE FROSTING
30g butter, softened
60g cream cheese, softened
1 teaspoon vanilla essence
1 1/2 cups (240g) icing
  sugar mixture

1 Position oven shelves; preheat oven to moderate. Grease deep 23cm-square cake pan, line base with baking paper.

2 Drain pineapple over medium bowl, pressing with spoon to extract as much syrup as possible. Reserve 1/4 cup (60ml) syrup.

3 Sift flours, soda, spices and sugar into large bowl. Using wooden spoon, stir in drained pineapple, reserved syrup, coconut, banana, egg and oil; pour into prepared pan.

4 Bake cake in moderate oven about 40 minutes. Stand cake 5 minutes then turn onto wire rack; turn cake top-side up to cool.

5 Spread cold cake with cream cheese frosting.

cream cheese frosting Beat butter, cream cheese and essence in small bowl with electric mixer until light and fluffy; gradually beat in icing sugar.

SERVES 12

per serving 21.1g fat; 1836kJ

Mashing overripe banana with a fork

Draining pineapple well

Pouring cake mixture into prepared pan

TIPS Use a light blended vegetable oil, such as corn, safflower or canola.

• Use commercially made cream cheese, such as full-fat Philadelphia.

• The pineapple must be well drained; too much syrup will give you a heavy cake. Canned crushed pineapple gives better results than blended or processed fresh or canned pieces or slices.

• The bananas you use must be overripe: the fruit's natural starch is converted to sugar during ripening, and it's this natural sugar that contributes to the correct balance of ingredients.

• Overripe bananas freeze well. Place fruit too ripe to be palatable straight into your freezer: the skin will blacken, but the fruit inside is fine to use.

• Toasted shredded coconut is good sprinkled over the frosting.

storage Cake will keep for up to 3 days in an airtight container in the refrigerator.

Frosted or unfrosted, the cake can be frozen for up to 3 months.

carrot cake with lemon cream cheese frosting

PREPARATION TIME 35 MINUTES • BAKING TIME 1 HOUR 15 MINUTES

You need approximately 3 large carrots (540g) for this recipe.

1 cup (250ml) vegetable oil
$1^{1}/_{3}$ cups (250g) firmly packed brown sugar
3 eggs
3 cups firmly packed, coarsely grated carrot
1 cup (120g) coarsely chopped walnuts
$2^{1}/_{2}$ cups (375g) self-raising flour
$^{1}/_{2}$ teaspoon bicarbonate of soda
2 teaspoons mixed spice

LEMON CREAM CHEESE FROSTING
30g butter, softened
80g cream cheese, softened
1 teaspoon finely grated lemon rind
$1^{1}/_{2}$ cups (240g) icing sugar mixture

1 Position oven shelves; preheat oven to moderate. Grease deep 22cm-round cake pan, line base with baking paper.

2 Beat oil, sugar and eggs in small bowl with electric mixer until thick and creamy.

3 Transfer mixture to large bowl; using wooden spoon, stir in carrot and nuts then sifted dry ingredients. Pour mixture into prepared pan.

4 Bake cake in moderate oven about $1^{1}/_{4}$ hours. Stand cake 5 minutes then turn onto wire rack; turn cake top-side up to cool.

5 Spread cold cake with lemon cream cheese frosting.

lemon cream cheese frosting Beat butter, cream cheese and rind in small bowl with electric mixer until light and fluffy; gradually beat in icing sugar.

SERVES 12

per serving 32.1g fat; 2377kJ

TIPS Cover cake loosely with foil during baking if it starts to overbrown.

• Use a light blended vegetable oil, such as corn, safflower or canola.

• Pecans can be substituted for walnuts.

• Use commercially made cream cheese, such as full-fat Philadelphia.

storage Cake will keep up to 3 days if refrigerated in an airtight container.

Frosted or unfrosted, the cake can be frozen for up to 3 months.

Coarsely grating carrots

Transferring mixture to a large bowl

Adding icing sugar to frosting mixture

coco-berry-nut cake

PREPARATION TIME 20 MINUTES • BAKING TIME 50 MINUTES

*This lusciously moist cake comes straight from the oven with its own baked-on topping
– but a dollop of whipped cream on a warm piece won't go astray!*

250g butter, softened
1 teaspoon vanilla essence
1¹/₄ cups (275g) caster sugar
3 eggs
²/₃ cup (100g) plain flour
1 cup (150g) self-raising flour
1/₂ cup (55g) hazelnut meal
150g frozen raspberries

COCONUT TOPPING
1/₃ cup (50g) plain flour
2 tablespoons caster sugar
40g butter
**1/₃ cup (15g) flaked coconut,
   chopped coarsely**

1   Position oven shelves; preheat oven to moderate. Grease deep
    23cm-square cake pan; line base with baking paper.

2   Beat butter, essence and sugar in small bowl with electric mixer
    until light and fluffy; beat in eggs, one at a time, until just combined
    between additions.

3   Transfer mixture to large bowl; using wooden spoon, stir in flours
    and hazelnut meal.

4   Spread mixture evenly into prepared pan; sprinkle evenly with raspberries,
    then coconut topping.

5   Bake cake in moderate oven about 50 minutes. Stand cake 5 minutes then
    turn onto wire rack; turn cake top-side up to cool.

coconut topping   Combine flour and sugar in small bowl. Rub in butter;
using fork, stir in coconut.

SERVES 12

per serving   25.1g fat; 1763kJ

Transferring creamed mixture to larger bowl

Rubbing butter into coconut topping mixture

Sprinkling coconut topping over raspberries

TIPS Cover cake loosely with foil if it starts to overbrown during baking.

• It is best to use still-frozen raspberries. You can also use fresh raspberries, but avoid using very large berries because they have a tendency to sink into the cake mixture.

• Fresh or frozen blueberries can be substituted for raspberries.

• Almond meal can be substituted for hazelnut meal.

storage Cake will keep for 1 day in an airtight container in the refrigerator.

Cake can be frozen for up to 3 months.

banana cake with passionfruit icing

PREPARATION TIME 35 MINUTES • BAKING TIME 50 MINUTES

You need approximately 2 large overripe bananas (460g) for this recipe.

125g butter, softened
3/4 cup (150g) firmly packed
   brown sugar
2 eggs
1 1/2 cups (225g) self-raising flour
1/2 teaspoon bicarbonate of soda
1 teaspoon mixed spice
1 cup mashed banana
1/2 cup (120g) sour cream
1/4 cup (60ml) milk

PASSIONFRUIT ICING
1 1/2 cups (240g) icing
   sugar mixture
1 teaspoon soft butter
2 tablespoons passionfruit
   pulp, approximately

1 Position oven shelves; preheat oven to moderate. Grease 15cm x 25cm loaf pan; line base with baking paper.

2 Beat butter and sugar in small bowl with electric mixer until light and fluffy. Beat in eggs, one at a time, until combined. Transfer mixture to large bowl; using wooden spoon, stir in sifted dry ingredients, banana, cream and milk. Spread mixture into prepared pan.

3 Bake cake in moderate oven about 50 minutes. Stand cake 5 minutes then turn onto wire rack; turn cake top-side up to cool.

4 Spread cold cake with passionfruit icing.

passionfruit icing Place icing sugar in small heatproof bowl, stir in butter and enough pulp to give a firm paste. Stir over hot water until icing is of spreading consistency, taking care not to overheat; use immediately.

SERVES 10

per serving 17.1g fat; 1724kJ

Spreading mixture into prepared pan

Pouring passionfruit icing over cake

TIPS It is important that the bananas you use are overripe: not only do they mash easily but, if they are underripe, the cake will be too heavy.

• A banana's natural starch is converted to sugar during the ripening process, and it's this natural sugar that contributes to the correct balance of ingredients. The cake also develops a crusty edge due to this sugar content.

• The icing must be made in a heatproof bowl, preferably one made from glass or china. Stand the bowl over a saucepan of barely simmering water or in a sink filled with hot water; stir icing until it is just warmed and thin enough to pour easily. Use the icing immediately because it will set very quickly.

• This cake can also be baked in a deep 20cm-round pan, its base lined with baking paper, in a moderate oven for about 1 hour and 5 minutes.

storage Cake will keep for up to 3 days in an airtight container.

Unfrosted cake can be frozen for up to 3 months.

almond and strawberry friands

PREPARATION TIME 20 MINUTES • BAKING TIME 25 MINUTES

Friands gain their fine texture from the icing sugar and almond meal that partly replace the usual flour. You can use fresh or frozen berries for this recipe.

6 egg whites
185g butter, melted
1 cup (125g) almond meal
1¹/₂ cups (240g) icing
** sugar mixture**
¹/₂ cup (75g) plain flour
100g strawberries, sliced thinly

1 Position shelves in oven; preheat oven to moderately hot. Grease 12 (¹/₂ cup/125ml) rectangular or oval friand pans, stand on oven tray.

2 Place egg whites in medium bowl; whisk lightly with a fork until combined. Add butter, almond meal, icing sugar and flour to bowl; using wooden spoon, stir until just combined. Divide mixture among prepared pans; top with strawberry slices.

3 Bake friands in moderately hot oven about 25 minutes. Stand friands in pans 5 minutes then turn onto wire rack; turn friands top-side up to cool.

4 Serve warm, or at room temperature, dusted with a little extra sifted icing sugar.

MAKES 12

per friand 17.8g fat; 1143kJ

A variety of suitable pans for friands

Placing strawberry slices on friand mixture

TIPS You can use frozen egg whites, thawed, in this recipe. These are readily available in supermarkets.

• If using frozen berries, use them unthawed to minimise their colour "bleeding" into mixture.

• The traditional friand pan is oval; however, small loaf-shape pans, having a 1/2-cup (125ml) capacity, are also available from kitchen and cookware shops. These individual pans should be grouped on an oven tray before being placed in the oven to make them easy to handle. Alternatively, 6-, 8-, 9- and 12-hole friand pans are available from selected kitchen and cookware shops, or you could use muffin pans; each hole should have a 1/2-cup (125ml) capacity.

storage Friands are at their best made on the day of serving, but can be stored in an airtight container for up to 2 days.

Friands can be frozen for up to 3 months.

Friands can be thawed, individually wrapped in foil, in a moderate oven for about 15 minutes or in a microwave oven, unwrapped, on HIGH (100%) for about 30 seconds.

VARIATIONS

plain Omit strawberries; hazelnut meal can be substituted for almond meal.
per serving 17.8g fat; 1137kJ

blueberry Substitute 80g fresh or frozen blueberries for the strawberries.
per serving 17.8g fat; 1150kJ

banana Use hazelnut or almond meal; top each unbaked friand with a thin slice of banana.
per serving 18.3g fat; 1109kJ

raspberry and white chocolate Stir 100g coarsely chopped white chocolate into the egg-white mixture; substitute 150g fresh or frozen raspberries for the strawberries, and use almond or hazelnut meal. per serving 21.2g fat; 1355kJ

chocolate Stir 100g coarsely chopped dark chocolate into egg-white mixture; use almond or hazelnut meal. per serving 20.9g fat; 1326kJ

coffee Dissolve 2 teaspoons instant coffee powder in 2 teaspoons hot water, add to egg-white mixture; use hazelnut or almond meal, and top each unbaked friand with two whole coffee beans. per serving 19.2g fat; 1502kJ

lime coconut Stir 2 teaspoons finely grated lime rind, 1 tablespoon lime juice and 1/4 cup (20g) desiccated coconut into the egg-white mixture; sprinkle unbaked friands with 1/3 cup (15g) flaked coconut. per serving 19.7g fat; 1215kJ

TIPS It is important not to overmix muffin mixture; it should be slightly lumpy.

• If using frozen berries, use them unthawed, this will minimise "bleeding" of the colour into the mixture.

• To thaw frozen muffins, either place muffins on an oven tray covered with foil, or wrap individual muffins in foil; thaw in moderate oven about 20 minutes.

• Individual unwrapped muffins can be thawed in a microwave oven on HIGH (100%) for about 30 seconds.

• Traditionally, these American muffins are served warm with butter.

storage Muffins are at their best made on the day of serving; however, they can be stored in an airtight container for up to 2 days.

Muffins can be frozen either individually wrapped in foil or together in a sealed container for up to 3 months.

raspberry and coconut muffins

PREPARATION TIME 10 MINUTES • BAKING TIME 20 MINUTES

2^1/$_2$ cups (375g) self-raising flour
90g butter, chopped
1 cup (220g) caster sugar
1^1/$_4$ cups (310ml) buttermilk
1 egg, beaten lightly
^{1}/$_3$ cup (30g) desiccated coconut
150g fresh or frozen raspberries
2 tablespoons shredded coconut

1 Position oven shelves; preheat oven to moderately hot. Grease 12-hole (^{1}/$_3$ cup/80ml) muffin pan.

2 Place flour in large bowl; using fingertips, rub in butter. Add sugar, buttermilk, egg, desiccated coconut and raspberries; using fork, mix until just combined.

3 Divide mixture among holes of prepared pan; sprinkle with shredded coconut.

4 Bake in moderately hot oven about 20 minutes. Stand muffins 5 minutes then turn onto wire rack to cool.

MAKES 12

per muffin 9.8g fat; 1165kJ

Stirring ingredients together

Sprinkling coconut over muffin mixture

christmas cakes

fruity almond ring

PREPARATION TIME 20 MINUTES (plus standing time)
BAKING TIME 1 HOUR 30 MINUTES

2^1/$_4$ **cups (320g) sultanas**
^{3}/$_4$ **cup (180ml) orange juice**
185g butter, softened
2 teaspoons finely grated orange rind
^{1}/$_3$ **cup (75g) demerara sugar**
^{1}/$_3$ **cup (75g) caster sugar**
3 eggs
^{2}/$_3$ **cup (100g) plain flour**
^{1}/$_3$ **cup (50g) self-raising flour**
1 cup (180g) whole blanched almonds
^{1}/$_3$ **cup (115g) orange marmalade**

1 Combine sultanas and juice in large bowl, cover; stand overnight.

2 Position oven shelves; preheat oven to slow. Grease deep 20cm ring pan;
   line base with baking paper.

3 Beat butter, rind and sugars in small bowl with electric mixer until
   light and fluffy. Add eggs, one at a time, beating well between additions.
   Mixture may curdle at this point but will come together later.

4 Using wooden spoon, stir creamed mixture into sultana mixture
   with flours. Spoon mixture into prepared pan; sprinkle evenly
   with almonds.

5 Bake cake in slow oven about 1^1/$_2$ hours.

6 Heat marmalade in small saucepan without boiling; strain into heatproof
   jug. Brush hot cake with hot marmalade; cool cake, uncovered, in pan.

SERVES 16

per serving 16.9g fat; 1315kJ

Spooning mixture into prepared pan

Brushing hot cake with hot marmalade

TIPS This cake can be baked in two 8cm x 25cm bar cake pans, bases lined with baking paper, in a slow oven for about 1 hour and 20 minutes.

• Cover cake loosely with foil during baking if it starts to overbrown.

• Give the cake quarter turns several times during baking if browning unevenly.

• Marmalade can be warmed in the microwave oven.

• Apricot jam can be substituted for marmalade.

storage Wrap cold cake tightly in plastic wrap to keep airtight, then in foil. Wrapped cake can be kept in a cool dark place for about 2 weeks; however, if the climate is humid, it is safest to keep the cake in a sealed plastic bag or tightly sealed container in the refrigerator.

Cake can be frozen for up to 3 months.

super-moist rich fruit cake

PREPARATION TIME 30 MINUTES (plus standing time) • BAKING TIME 4 HOURS

This cake is very moist, due to the proportion of fruit to flour, which gives it a similar texture to Christmas pudding. Great as a family dessert with custard or, traditionally, for more special occasions such as weddings and 21sts.

2^1/$_4$ cups (380g) raisins, chopped coarsely
3 cups (500g) sultanas
^{3}/$_4$ cup (110g) currants
1 cup (250g) quartered red glacé cherries
1^1/$_2$ cups (250g) coarsely chopped seeded prunes
^{1}/$_3$ cup (115g) honey
^{1}/$_2$ cup (125ml) brandy
250g butter, softened
1 cup (200g) firmly packed black sugar
5 eggs
1^1/$_4$ cups (185g) plain flour
2 tablespoons brandy, extra

1 Combine fruit, honey and brandy in large bowl, mix well with one hand, cover; stand overnight.

2 Position oven shelves, preheat oven to slow. Line base and sides of deep 19cm-square cake pan with three thicknesses baking paper, bringing paper 5cm above sides of pan.

3 Beat butter and sugar in small bowl with electric mixer until just combined; beat in eggs, one at a time, until just combined between additions. Mixture may curdle at this point but will come together later.

4 Add creamed mixture to fruit mixture with flour; mix thoroughly with one hand.

5 Drop dollops of mixture into corners of pan to hold paper in position; spread remaining mixture into pan.

6 Drop cake pan from a height of about 15cm onto bench to settle mixture into pan and to break any large air bubbles; level surface of cake mixture with wet metal spatula.

7 Bake cake in slow oven about 4 hours.

8 Remove cake from oven, brush with extra brandy. Cover pan tightly with foil; cool cake in pan.

SERVES 48

per serving 5g fat; 719kJ

Chopping prunes with scissors

Beating butter and sugar until just combined

Scraping creamed mixture into fruit mixture

Using hand to mix ingredients

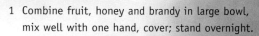

TIPS This cake can also be baked in deep 22cm-round cake pan.

• Rum, sherry or your favourite liqueur can be substituted for the brandy.

• The fruit mixture can be made up to a month before required and stored in a cool, dark place – the refrigerator is ideal.

• You can use dark brown or brown sugar rather than black if you prefer.

• Cover cake loosely with foil during baking if it starts to overbrown. Give the cake quarter turns several times during baking to avoid it browning unevenly.

• Because it is quite soft, this cake is best cut cold, after refrigeration.

storage Covered cake in pan will go from oven to room temperature in about 24 hours. Remove cake from pan by turning cake upside down onto bench, carefully peeling away lining paper from sides of cake but leaving base lining paper in place. Wrap cake tightly in plastic wrap to keep airtight, then in foil. Wrapped cake can be kept in a cool dark place for about 12 months; however, if the climate is humid, it is safest to keep the cake in a sealed plastic bag or tightly sealed container in the refrigerator.

Cake can be frozen for up to 12 months.

festive fruit and nut cake

PREPARATION TIME 35 MINUTES • BAKING TIME 1 HOUR 45 MINUTES

Also known as a Stained Glass, American, Canadian or Jewel cake, this easy- and quick-to-make cake had its origins in the New World. Refrigerating it helps make cutting a breeze, and it can be sliced especially finely if you use a sharp serrated or electric knife. The topping is an optional extra, but it looks and tastes wonderful.

3 rings (85g) glacé pineapple, chopped coarsely
1/2 cup (125g) glacé apricots, chopped coarsely
1 1/2 cups (250g) seeded dried dates
1/2 cup (105g) red glacé cherries
1/2 cup (105g) green glacé cherries
3/4 cup (120g) whole blanched almonds
1 1/2 cups (250g) brazil nuts
2 eggs
1/2 cup (100g) firmly packed brown sugar
1 tablespoon dark rum
90g butter, softened
1/3 cup (50g) plain flour
1/4 cup (35g) self-raising flour

FRUIT AND NUT TOPPING
4 rings (125g) glacé pineapple, chopped coarsely
1/4 cup (50g) red glacé cherries, halved
1/4 cup (50g) green glacé cherries, halved
2/3 cup (110g) brazil nuts
2/3 cup (110g) whole blanched almonds

GLAZE
1 1/2 teaspoons gelatine
1 tablespoon water

1 Position oven shelves; preheat oven to slow. Grease deep 20cm ring pan; line base and side with baking paper.

2 Combine fruit and nuts in large bowl.

3 Beat eggs in small bowl with electric mixer until thick and creamy; add sugar, rum and butter, beat until just combined.

4 Using wooden spoon stir egg mixture into fruit mixture with flours. Spoon mixture into prepared pan; press firmly into pan with fingers.

5 Arrange fruit and nut topping over cake mixture.

6 Bake cake in slow oven 1 hour; cover loosely with foil, bake about 45 minutes. Stand cake in pan 10 minutes then turn onto wire rack; turn top-side up ready to glaze.

7 Brush glaze evenly over fruit and nut topping.

fruit and nut topping Combine fruit and nuts in medium bowl; using one hand, mix well.

glaze Combine gelatine and the water in cup, stand in small saucepan of simmering water; stir gelatine mixture until dissolved, stand 3 minutes.

SERVES 24

per serving 19.2g fat; 1331kJ

Beating eggs until thick and creamy

Combining egg and fruit mixtures with flours

Pressing mixture into cake pan

Glazing baked cake

TIPS Give the cake quarter turns several times during baking if it is browning unevenly.

• This cake can also be baked in two lined 8cm x 25cm bar cake pans.

• Fruit should be cut into chunks the same size as the brazil nuts.

storage Wrap cold cake tightly in plastic wrap to keep airtight, then in foil. Wrapped cake can be kept in a sealed plastic bag or tightly sealed container in the refrigerator for up to 1 month.

Cake can be frozen for up to 3 months.

brandied date cake

PREPARATION TIME 25 MINUTES • BAKING TIME 1 HOUR 30 MINUTES

The addition of the cream cheese gives this luscious cake an especially moist, rich quality.

90g butter, softened
125g cream cheese, softened
1¼ cups (250g) firmly packed brown sugar
3 eggs
½ cup (75g) plain flour
½ cup (75g) self-raising flour
¼ cup (60ml) brandy
2⅓ cups (380g) coarsely chopped seeded dried dates
½ cup (85g) mixed peel
1 tablespoon brandy, extra

1 Position oven shelves; preheat oven to slow. Line base and side of deep 20cm-round cake pan with three thicknesses baking paper, bringing paper 5cm above edge of pan.

2 Beat butter, cheese, sugar, eggs, flours and brandy in large bowl on low speed with electric mixer until ingredients are combined. Beat on medium speed until mixture is smooth and changed in colour.

3 Using wooden spoon, mix in dates and peel. Spoon mixture into prepared pan, level surface of cake mixture with wet metal spatula.

4 Bake cake in slow oven about 1½ hours.

5 Brush hot cake with extra brandy. Cover pan tightly with foil; cool cake in pan. When cake is cold, and just before serving, decorate if desired by cutting a star shape out of paper; centre paper star on cake then dust top of cake with sifted icing sugar, carefully remove paper star.

SERVES 22

per serving 6.1g fat; 787kJ

TIPS If both butter and eggs are at room temperature, this will help prevent the mixture from curdling.

• Use commercially made packaged cream cheese, such as full-fat Philadelphia.

• Cover cake loosely with foil during baking if it starts to overbrown.

• Give the cake quarter turns several times during baking if browning unevenly.

storage Remove cold cake from pan, wrap cake tightly in plastic wrap to keep airtight, then in foil. Wrapped cake can be kept in a cool dark place for about 2 weeks; however, if the climate is humid, keep the cake in a sealed plastic bag or tightly sealed container in the refrigerator.

Cake can be frozen for up to 3 months.

Beating ingredients until combined

Beating ingredients until changed in colour

Brushing hot cake with brandy

TIPS The cake mixture must be cold before stirring in eggs and dry ingredients. This is a great cake to start preparing a day ahead of baking; after the mixture cools, cover and allow to stand overnight. Do not refrigerate.

• Cover cake loosely with foil during baking if it starts to overbrown.

• Give the cake quarter turns several times during baking if browning unevenly.

• Sherry, brandy, whisky or your favourite liqueur can be substituted for rum.

storage Covered cake in pan will go from oven to room temperature in about 12 hours. Remove cake from pan by turning upside down onto bench and carefully peeling lining paper away from sides but leaving base paper in place. Wrap cake tightly in plastic wrap to keep airtight, then in foil. Wrapped cake can be kept in a cool, dark place for about 2 weeks; however, if the climate is humid, keep the cake in a sealed plastic bag or tightly sealed container in the refrigerator.

Cake can be frozen for up to 3 months.

Stirring ingredients over heat

Pouring mixture into prepared cake pan

boiled pineapple rum cake

PREPARATION TIME 20 MINUTES (plus cooling time)
BAKING TIME 2 HOURS

Pineapple and rum seem to have been made for one another, and this new take on an old favourite proves the point. This cake has particularly good keeping qualities because of the large amount of butter it contains.

440g can crushed pineapple in syrup
1kg (5 cups) mixed dried fruit
250g butter, chopped coarsely
1 cup (200g) firmly packed brown sugar
2 tablespoons orange marmalade
2 tablespoons dark rum
4 eggs, beaten lightly
1²/₃ cups (250g) plain flour
1/3 cup (50g) self-raising flour
1/2 teaspoon bicarbonate of soda
1 tablespoon dark rum, extra

1 Drain pineapple over large jug; discard 1/2-cup (125ml) of the syrup.

2 Combine pineapple, remaining syrup, fruit, butter, sugar, marmalade and rum in large saucepan. Using wooden spoon, stir over heat until butter melts and sugar dissolves; bring to a boil. Reduce heat; simmer, covered, 10 minutes. Cool to room temperature.

3 Position oven shelves; preheat oven to slow. Line base and side of deep 20cm-round cake pan with three thicknesses baking paper, bringing paper 5cm above edge of pan.

4 Using wooden spoon, stir egg and sifted dry ingredients into fruit mixture. Pour mixture into prepared pan.

5 Bake cake in slow oven about 2 hours. Brush hot cake with extra rum. Cover pan tightly with foil; cool cake in pan. Decorate with toffee stars, if desired.

SERVES 28

per serving 8.5g fat; 1053kJ

Chopping nuts finely

Stirring in sifted dry ingredients and milk

Sprinkling cake mixture with nut topping

mixed nut cake

PREPARATION TIME 25 MINUTES • BAKING TIME 1 HOUR 15 MINUTES

A Greek New Year's cake called vasilopita, this recipe is traditionally made with a single coin baked into it, legend having it that the person who is served the slice containing the coin will have good luck in the coming year.

125g butter, softened
1 teaspoon finely grated lemon rind
1¼ cups (275g) caster sugar
3 eggs
½ cup (75g) self-raising flour
1 cup (150g) plain flour
¼ teaspoon bicarbonate of soda
½ cup (125ml) milk
1 tablespoon lemon juice
2 tablespoons pistachios, chopped finely
2 tablespoons walnuts, chopped finely
2 tablespoons slivered almonds, chopped finely
2 teaspoons icing sugar mixture

NUT TOPPING
2 tablespoons pistachios, chopped coarsely
2 tablespoons walnuts, chopped coarsely
2 tablespoons slivered almonds

1 Position oven shelves; preheat oven to moderate. Line base and side of deep 22cm-round cake pan with baking paper.

2 Combine butter, rind and sugar in small bowl; beat with electric mixer until light and fluffy. Add eggs, one at a time, beating well between additions. Mixture will curdle at this point but will come together later.

3 Using wooden spoon, stir in sifted dry ingredients and milk, in two batches; stir in juice and nuts.

4 Spoon mixture into prepared pan, level surface of cake mixture with wet metal spatula.

5 Bake cake in moderate oven 30 minutes. Cover cake loosely with foil; bake about 45 minutes.

6 Stand cake in pan 5 minutes then turn onto wire rack; turn top-side up to cool. Dust cake with sifted icing sugar before serving.

nut topping Combine all ingredients in small bowl.

SERVES 14

per serving 14.7g fat; 1176kJ

TIPS This cake can be baked in a deep 19cm-square cake pan.

• Mix and match varieties and quantities of nuts to suit your taste. All nuts can be stored in an airtight container in the freezer; they can be used directly from the freezer.

storage Store cake in an airtight container for up to 2 days.

Cake can be frozen for up to 3 months.

quick-mix low-fat fruit cakes

PREPARATION TIME 25 MINUTES (plus standing time) • BAKING TIME 1 HOUR 45 MINUTES

These cakes make a great gift for any weight-conscious friends or family members because of their comparatively low fat content.

4 cups (750g) mixed dried fruit
1/2 cup (105g) red glacé cherries, quartered
2/3 cup (150g) firmly packed brown sugar
11/2 cups (375ml) apple juice
2 egg whites, beaten lightly
1/4 cup (60ml) vegetable oil
1/3 cup (80ml) skim milk
2 tablespoons brandy
21/4 cups (360g) wholemeal self-raising flour
1 teaspoon mixed spice
1/2 teaspoon ground ginger
1 tablespoon brandy, extra

TIPS Cake mixture can also be baked in a deep 19cm-square or deep 22cm-round cake pan; baking time will increase to about 21/4 hours. Line base and sides of larger pans with three thicknesses baking paper, bringing paper 5cm above edge of pan.

• Rum, sherry or your favourite liqueur can be substituted for the brandy.

• Use a light-flavoured all-purpose vegetable oil, such as canola, in this recipe.

storage Wrap cakes tightly in plastic wrap to keep airtight; refrigerate in airtight container for up to 1 month. Cakes can be frozen for up to 3 months.

1 Combine fruit, cherries, sugar and juice in large bowl, cover; stand overnight.

2 Position oven shelves; preheat oven to slow. Grease seven 8.5cm-round cake pans; line bases with three thicknesses baking paper.

3 Using wooden spoon, stir egg white, oil, milk, brandy and sifted dry ingredients into fruit mixture. Divide mixture evenly among prepared pans.

4 Bake cakes in slow oven about 13/4 hours. Brush hot cakes with extra brandy. Cover pans tightly with foil; cool cakes in pans.

5 Decorate cakes with star shapes cut from rolled almond paste, if desired; position stars on cakes, decorate with silver, gold or coloured cachous.

SERVES 21

per serving 3.3g fat; 959kJ

Sifting dry ingredients over fruit mixture

Dividing cake mixture among pans

Mixing in flour, spice and sherry

Dropping mixture into corners of cake pan

Levelling surface of cake mixture

beginners' christmas cake

PREPARATION TIME 30 MINUTES • BAKING TIME 3 HOURS

The perfect cake with which to start your baking career! Make it ahead of time and keep it for Christmas, or bake it at the last minute for an impromptu engagement celebration – remember that this cake needs a day to come to room temperature.

250g butter, softened
1¼ cups (250g) firmly packed
   brown sugar
4 eggs
2 tablespoons orange marmalade
1.5kg (7¾ cups) mixed
   dried fruit
1½ cups (225g) plain flour
½ cup (75g) self-raising flour
2 teaspoons mixed spice
½ cup (125ml) sweet sherry
¼ cup (30g) blanched
   whole almonds
2 tablespoons sweet sherry, extra

1 Position oven shelves; preheat oven to slow. Line base and sides of deep 19cm-square cake pan with three thicknesses baking paper, bringing paper 5cm above sides of pan.

2 Beat butter and sugar in small bowl with electric mixer until just combined; beat in eggs, one at a time, until just combined between additions. Mixture may curdle at this point but will come together later.

3 Scrape mixture into large bowl; add marmalade and fruit, mix thoroughly with one hand.

4 Sift flours and spice over mixture; add sherry, mix well.

5 Drop dollops of mixture into corners of pan to hold paper in position; spread remaining mixture into pan.

6 Drop cake pan from a height of about 15cm onto bench to settle mixture into pan and to break any large air bubbles; level surface of cake mixture with wet metal spatula, decorate top with almonds.

7 Bake cake in slow oven about 3 hours. Remove cake from oven; brush top with extra sherry. Cover pan tightly with foil; cool cake in pan.

SERVES 36

per serving 7.2g fat; 1006kJ

TIPS If both butter and eggs are at room temperature, this will help avoid the mixture curdling.

• Buy fruit already mixed, or mix your own to suit your taste. All fruit should be chopped to the size of a sultana.

• Nuts can be added to the fruit mixture, if you like; 125g blanched whole almonds, chopped coarsely, is an ideal amount.

• You can use dark brown or black sugar rather than brown sugar for a more richly coloured cake.

• Rum, brandy or your favourite liqueur can be substituted for the sherry. Cointreau and Grand Marnier work especially well with this recipe.

• This cake can also be baked in a deep 22cm-round cake pan.

• Cover cake loosely with foil during baking if it starts to overbrown. Give the cake quarter turns several times during baking to avoid uneven browning.

storage Covered cake in pan will go from oven to room temperature in about 24 hours. Remove cake from pan by turning cake upside down onto bench and carefully peeling lining paper away from sides but leaving base paper in place. Wrap cake tightly in plastic wrap to keep airtight, then in foil. Wrapped cake can be kept in a cool, dark place for about 3 months; however, if your climate is humid, keep the cake in a sealed plastic bag or tightly sealed container in the refrigerator.

Cake can be frozen for up to 12 months.

Coarsely chopping figs with scissors

Beating ingredients until combined

Beating ingredients until changed in colour

coconut apricot cake

PREPARATION TIME 25 MINUTES • BAKING TIME 1 HOUR 30 MINUTES

A light alternative to the other rich or heavy Christmas cakes, this version is wonderfully moist and beautifully coconut-flavoured.

185g butter, softened
3/4 cup (165g) caster sugar
3 eggs
1 cup (90g) desiccated coconut
1/2 cup (75g) plain flour
1/2 cup (75g) self-raising flour
1/2 cup (125ml) coconut milk
1 cup (190g) coarsely chopped dried figs
3/4 cup (185g) coarsely chopped glacé apricots
2/3 cup (110g) sultanas

1 Position oven shelves; preheat oven to slow. Line base and side of deep 20cm-round cake pan with three thicknesses baking paper, extending paper 5cm above edge of pan.

2 Beat butter, sugar, eggs, coconut, flours and milk in large bowl on low speed with electric mixer until ingredients are combined. Beat on medium speed until mixture is changed in colour. Using wooden spoon, stir in fruit; spread mixture into prepared pan.

3 Bake cake in slow oven about 1^1/$_2$ hours.

4 Cover pan tightly with foil; cool cake in pan.

SERVES 22

per serving 11.6g fat; 909kJ

TIPS Cover cake loosely with foil during baking if it starts to overbrown.

• Give the cake quarter turns several times during baking if browning unevenly.

• Glacé figs can be substituted for dried figs, and glacé pineapple can be substituted for both the apricots or figs.

storage Remove cake from pan; wrap cake tightly in plastic wrap to keep airtight, then in foil. Wrapped cake can be kept in cool, dark place for about 2 weeks; however, if the climate is humid, keep the cake in a sealed plastic bag or tightly sealed container in the refrigerator.

Cake can be frozen for up to 3 months.

cherry almond cake

PREPARATION TIME 20 MINUTES (plus standing time) • BAKING TIME 1 HOUR 30 MINUTES

With its use of the season's traditional green and red colour combination, this festive cake is perfect for Christmas.

Using scissors, quarter cherries

Adding eggs one at a time

Levelling cake mixture with wet spatula

185g butter, softened
1 cup (220g) caster sugar
1 teaspoon almond essence
3 eggs
$^1/_2$ cup (105g) red glacé cherries, quartered
$^1/_3$ cup (70g) green glacé cherries, quartered
1 cup (160g) sultanas
$^2/_3$ cup (90g) slivered almonds
1 cup (150g) plain flour
$^1/_2$ cup (75g) self-raising flour
$^1/_3$ cup (80ml) milk

1 Position oven shelves; preheat oven to moderately slow. Line base and side of deep 20cm-round cake pan with three thicknesses baking paper, extending paper 5cm above edge of pan.

2 Combine butter, sugar and essence in small bowl; beat with electric mixer until light and fluffy. Add eggs, one at a time, beating well between additions. Mixture may curdle at this point but will come together later.

3 Combine cherries, sultanas and nuts in large bowl; using wooden spoon, stir in creamed mixture, flours and milk. Spread mixture into prepared pan, level surface with wet metal spatula.

4 Bake cake in moderately slow oven about 1$^1/_2$ hours.

5 Cover pan tightly with foil; cool cake in pan.

SERVES 22

per serving 10.2g fat; 918kJ

TIPS Cover cake loosely with foil during baking if it starts to overbrown.

• Give the cake quarter turns several times during baking to help to avoid it browning unevenly.

• Almond essence is available from supermarkets and health food stores.

storage Remove cake from pan; wrap cake tightly in plastic wrap to keep airtight, then in foil. Wrapped cake can be kept in a cool, dark place for about 2 weeks; however, if the climate is humid, keep the cake in a sealed plastic bag or tightly sealed container in the refrigerator.

Cake can be frozen for up to 3 months.

dessert cakes

raspberry hazelnut cake

PREPARATION TIME 30 MINUTES • BAKING TIME 1 HOUR 30 MINUTES

One of our favourites, this fabulous dessert cake is certain to become one of yours too. It's also a good cake to use as a wedding, engagement or birthday cake.

250g butter, softened
2 cups (440g) caster sugar
6 eggs
1 cup (150g) plain flour
1/2 cup (75g) self-raising flour
1 cup (110g) hazelnut meal
2/3 cup (160g) sour cream
300g fresh or frozen raspberries

MASCARPONE CREAM
250g mascarpone cheese
1/4 cup (40g) icing sugar mixture
2 tablespoons Frangelico
1/2 cup (120g) sour cream
1/2 cup (75g) roasted hazelnuts, chopped finely

TIPS If using frozen raspberries, don't thaw them: frozen berries are less likely to "bleed" into the cake mixture.

• Any berry of a similar size to raspberries can be used in this cake.

• Any nut, such as almonds, pecans or walnuts, can be substituted for the hazelnut meal; blend or process whole roasted nuts until fine.

• Choose a liqueur to complement the flavour of the nuts. A good combination would be amaretto with blueberries, almond meal and roasted chopped almond kernels.

storage Unfrosted cake will keep for up to 3 days in an airtight container at room temperature, if you live in a cool climate.

Cake can be frosted the day before required and stored in the refrigerator.

Unfrosted cake can be frozen for up to 3 months.

1 Position oven shelves; preheat oven to moderate. Grease deep 22cm-round cake pan; line base and side with baking paper.

2 Beat butter and sugar in medium bowl with electric mixer until light and fluffy; add eggs, one at a time, beating until just combined between additions. Mixture will curdle at this stage, but will come together later.

3 Transfer mixture to large bowl; using wooden spoon, stir in flours, hazelnut meal, sour cream and raspberries. Spread mixture into prepared pan.

4 Bake cake in moderate oven about 1½ hours. Stand cake 10 minutes; turn onto wire rack, turn top-side up to cool.

5 Place cake on serving plate. Using metal spatula, spread cake all over with mascarpone cream.

mascarpone cream Combine mascarpone, icing sugar, liqueur and sour cream in medium bowl. Using wooden spoon, stir until smooth; stir in nuts.

SERVES 12

per serving 50.6g fat; 3012kJ

Adding eggs to creaming mixture

Stirring raspberries into cake mixture

Combining ingredients for mascarpone cream

almond meringue cake

PREPARATION TIME 30 MINUTES • BAKING TIME 30 MINUTES

The combined textures of the soft cake, crisp meringue, crunchy nuts, rich berries and billows of whipped cream make this dessert-cake manna from heaven. It's best made on the day of serving.

125g butter, softened
1/2 cup (110g) caster sugar
3 eggs, separated
1 cup (150g) self-raising flour
1/3 cup (35g) cocoa powder
1/2 cup (125ml) buttermilk
1/2 cup (120g) sour cream
2/3 cup (150g) caster sugar, extra
2 tablespoons flaked almonds
2/3 cup (160ml) thickened cream
1 tablespoon icing sugar mixture
150g raspberries

Stirring ingredients together

Sprinkling meringue with almonds

Carefully turning cakes top-side up to cool

Sprinkling raspberries evenly over cream

1 Position oven shelves; preheat oven to moderate. Grease two deep 22cm-round cake pans; line bases with baking paper.

2 Beat butter, sugar and egg yolks in medium bowl with electric mixer until light and fluffy. Using wooden spoon, stir in combined sifted flour and cocoa, then combined buttermilk and sour cream.

3 Divide mixture evenly between prepared pans.

4 Beat egg whites in small bowl with electric mixer until soft peaks form; gradually add extra sugar, 1 tablespoon at a time, beating until sugar dissolves between additions. Divide meringue mixture evenly over cake mixture in pans; using metal spatula, spread meringue so cake mixture is completely covered. Sprinkle nuts over the meringue on one of the cakes.

5 Bake cakes in moderate oven 10 minutes. Cover pans loosely with foil; bake about 20 minutes. Discard foil; stand cakes in pans 5 minutes then turn onto wire racks. Quickly and carefully turn cakes top-side up to cool.

6 Beat cream and icing sugar in small bowl with rotary or electric mixer until firm peaks form. Place cake without almonds on serving plate; spread cream over top, sprinkle evenly with raspberries, top with remaining cake.

SERVES 12

per serving 20.7g fat; 1418kJ

TIPS These cakes are quite fragile. After turning cakes out of the pans, it's best to use two wire racks to turn them top-side up. If you have two 22cm springform tins, use them for baking these cakes: when you release the sides of the pans, there is no need to turn the cakes.

• When separating the eggs, take care to avoid any yolk getting into the whites or they will not beat to the correct meringue consistency.

storage Cake will keep for 1 day in an airtight container in the refrigerator.

white chocolate mud cake

PREPARATION TIME 30 MINUTES • BAKING TIME 2 HOURS

The white chocolate mud cake has rapidly ascended the ladder to the top of the special-occasion favourite-cake list.

250g butter, chopped coarsely
150g white chocolate,
  chopped coarsely
2 cups (440g) caster sugar
1 cup (250ml) milk
1¹/₂ cups (225g) plain flour
¹/₂ cup (75g) self-raising flour
1 teaspoon vanilla essence
2 eggs, beaten lightly

WHITE CHOCOLATE GANACHE
¹/₂ cup (125ml) cream
300g white chocolate,
  chopped coarsely

1 Position oven shelves; preheat oven to moderately slow. Grease deep 20cm-round cake pan; line base and side with baking paper.

2 Combine butter, chocolate, sugar and milk in medium saucepan; using wooden spoon, stir over low heat, without boiling, until smooth. Transfer mixture to large bowl; cool 15 minutes.

3 Whisk in flours then essence and egg; pour mixture into prepared pan.

4 Bake cake in moderately slow oven 1 hour. Cover pan loosely with foil; bake about 1 hour. Discard foil, stand cake in pan 10 minutes then turn onto wire rack; turn top-side up to cool.

5 Place cake on serving plate, spread all over with white chocolate ganache.

white chocolate ganache Bring cream to a boil in small saucepan; pour over chocolate in small bowl, stir with wooden spoon until chocolate melts. Cover bowl; refrigerate, stirring occasionally, about 30 minutes or until ganache is of a spreadable consistency.

SERVES 12

per serving 37g fat; 2756kJ

Transferring chocolate mixture to large bowl

Whisking flours into chocolate mixture

Beating spreadable ganache

TIPS This cake has a high fat and sugar content, and therefore it can be difficult to determine if it is cooked. The method of testing with a skewer is not accurate; following the baking times provided is the best guide, plus the crust on the finished cake should feel quite thick and sugary.

• If you require a level cake, don't cool the cake top-side up. Turn it out so that the bottom becomes the top of cooled cake that you cover with ganache.

storage Unfrosted cake will keep for up to 1 week in an airtight container at room temperature.

Frosted cake will keep for up to 1 week in an airtight container in the refrigerator.

Unfrosted cake can be frozen for up to 3 months.

TIPS To successfully make this cake, it is vital that the egg yolk/sugar mixture is beaten until thick and that the egg whites are beaten only until soft peaks form. Overbeating will dry out the egg whites and make it difficult to fold them into the chocolate mixture.

• We used a large metal spoon for the folding process; a plastic spatula also works well.

• To test if this cake is cooked, touch it with your fingertips: it should feel slightly firm and springy.

storage Cake will keep for up to 8 hours in an airtight container in the refrigerator.

Unrolled and unfilled cake can be stored, covered with a piece of baking paper then a damp tea-towel, overnight in the refrigerator.

black forest roulade

PREPARATION TIME 20 MINUTES • BAKING TIME 10 MINUTES

This cake is almost a cross between a mousse and a fallen soufflé. It's a wonderfully impressive cake to present for dessert or with tea and coffee, but it must be made on the day of serving. This recipe does not contain flour.

Folding egg whites into chocolate mixture

Folding egg yolk mixture into chocolate mixture

Rolling cake

200g dark chocolate, chopped coarsely
¹/4 cup (60ml) hot water
1 teaspoon instant coffee powder
4 eggs, separated
¹/2 cup (110g) caster sugar
1 tablespoon caster sugar, extra
¹/2 cup (125ml) thickened cream
1 tablespoon kirsch

CHERRY FILLING
425g can seedless black cherries
3 teaspoons cornflour
1 tablespoon kirsch

1 Position oven shelves; preheat oven to moderate. Grease 25cm x 30cm swiss roll pan; line base with baking paper.

2 Combine chocolate, water and coffee in large heatproof bowl; sit bowl over saucepan of simmering water. Using wooden spoon, stir until chocolate melts then immediately remove bowl from pan to bench.

3 Beat egg yolks and sugar in small bowl with electric mixer until thick and creamy; this will take about 5 minutes. Using large metal spoon, fold egg mixture into warm chocolate mixture.

4 Beat egg whites in small bowl with electric mixer until soft peaks form. Using metal spoon, gently fold egg whites into chocolate mixture, in two batches. Spread mixture into prepared pan. Bake in moderate oven about 10 minutes.

5 Meanwhile, place large sheet of baking paper on board; sprinkle with extra sugar. Turn cake onto sugared baking paper; carefully remove lining paper, cover cake loosely with tea-towel. Cool cake to room temperature.

6 Beat cream and kirsch in small bowl with rotary or electric mixer until firm peaks form. Spread cake evenly with cooled cherry filling then spread kirsch cream over cherry mixture. Roll cake from a long side, using paper to lift and guide the roll; place on serving plate. Cover roll; refrigerate 30 minutes before serving.

cherry filling Drain cherries, reserving ¹/4 cup (60ml) of syrup. Using knife, chop cherries coarsely. Using wooden spoon, blend cornflour and reserved syrup in small saucepan. Add cherries; stir over heat until mixture boils and thickens. Remove from heat, stir in kirsch; cover surface of mixture with plastic wrap, cool to room temperature.

SERVES 6

per serving 20.7g fat; 1834kJ

caramel mud cake

PREPARATION TIME 20 MINUTES • BAKING TIME 1 HOUR 30 MINUTES

This cake is a twist on the normal dark- or white-chocolate mud cake, but is just as delicious.

Whisking in flours

Pouring mixture into prepared pan

Pouring cream over chocolate

185g butter, chopped coarsely
150g white chocolate,
 chopped coarsely
1 cup (200g) firmly
 packed brown sugar
1/3 cup (80ml) golden syrup
1 cup (250ml) milk
11/2 cups (225g) plain flour
1/2 cup (75g) self-raising flour
2 eggs, beaten lightly

WHITE CHOCOLATE GANACHE
1/2 cup (125ml) cream
300g white chocolate,
 chopped coarsely

1 Preheat oven to moderately slow. Grease deep 22cm-round cake pan; line base and side with baking paper.

2 Combine butter, chocolate, sugar, golden syrup and milk in medium saucepan; stir over low heat, without boiling, until smooth. Transfer mixture to large bowl; cool for 15 minutes.

3 Whisk in flours then egg; pour mixture into prepared pan.

4 Bake cake in moderately slow oven about 11/2 hours.

5 Stand cake in pan 10 minutes then turn onto wire rack; turn top-side up to cool.

6 Place cake on serving plate, spread cake all over with white chocolate ganache.

white chocolate ganache Bring cream to a boil in small saucepan; pour over chocolate in small bowl, stir with wooden spoon until chocolate melts. Cover bowl; refrigerate, stirring occasionally, about 30 minutes or until ganache is of a spreadable consistency.

SERVES 12

per serving 31.6g fat; 2321kJ

TIPS This cake has a high fat and sugar content, and therefore it can be difficult to determine if it is cooked. The method of testing with a skewer is not accurate; the baking times given are your best guide, plus the crust on the finished cake should feel quite thick and sugary.

• If you require a level cake, don't cool the cake top-side up. Turn it out so that the bottom becomes the top of cooled cake that you cover with ganache.

storage Unfrosted cake will keep for up to 1 week in an airtight container at room temperature.

Frosted cake will keep for up to 1 week in an airtight container in the refrigerator.

Unfrosted cake can be frozen for up to 3 months.

marmalade polenta cake

PREPARATION TIME 20 MINUTES • BAKING TIME 1 HOUR 15 MINUTES

A very pretty cake, this is best served warm with lemon mascarpone soon after it is made. Slightly painstaking to make and difficult to slice neatly (but well worth the effort), this cake doesn't actually contain marmalade as an ingredient (but its artful use of citrus rind strikes a similar visual chord).

Turning orange and lemon slices

Overlapping slices in prepared pan

Stirring ingredients together

Scraping mixture into prepared pan

3/4 cup (165g) caster sugar
1 1/4 cups (310ml) water
1 medium unpeeled orange (240g), sliced thinly
1 large unpeeled lemon (180g), sliced thinly
1/4 cup (60ml) water, extra
125g butter, softened
1 tablespoon finely grated lemon rind
1 cup (220g) caster sugar, extra
3 eggs
1/2 cup (60g) almond meal
1/2 cup (75g) plain flour
1/2 cup (75g) self-raising flour
3/4 cup (125g) polenta
1/3 cup (80g) sour cream
1/4 cup (60ml) lemon juice

LEMON MASCARPONE

1 cup (250g) mascarpone cheese
2 teaspoons finely grated lemon rind
1 tablespoon lemon juice
2 tablespoons caster sugar

1 Position oven shelves; preheat oven to moderate. Grease deep 20cm-round cake pan; line base and side with baking paper.

2 Combine sugar and the water in large frying pan; using wooden spoon, stir over heat, without boiling, until sugar dissolves. Bring to a boil, reduce heat; simmer, without stirring, uncovered, about 5 minutes or until syrup thickens slightly. Add orange and lemon slices; simmer gently, uncovered, about 7 minutes or until rind is tender, turning slices halfway through cooking time.

3 Remove rind mixture from heat; using tongs, lift alternate orange and lemon slices directly from syrup to cover base and side of prepared pan, slightly overlapping each slice. Reserve syrup.

4 Add the extra water to reserved syrup in pan; bring to a boil. Reduce heat; simmer, uncovered, without stirring, about 5 minutes or until syrup is a light honey colour. Pour hot syrup over orange and lemon slices.

5 Beat butter, rind and extra sugar in small bowl with electric mixer until light and fluffy. Beat in eggs, one at a time, until combined. Mixture will curdle, but will come together later.

6 Transfer mixture to large bowl; using wooden spoon, stir in almond meal, flours, polenta, sour cream and juice. Carefully spread mixture into prepared pan.

7 Bake cake in moderate oven about 1 1/4 hours. Stand cake 15 minutes then turn onto serving plate. Serve cake warm with lemon mascarpone.

lemon mascarpone Combine ingredients in small bowl; whisk until smooth.

SERVES 12

per serving 27.6g fat; 1900kJ

TIPS You'll find it best to make the citrus mixture in a large frying pan rather than a saucepan, so that the citrus slices fit in it in a single layer.

• Polenta is the coarsely ground yellow cornmeal use for making cornmeal muffins and cornbread; it gives this cake a particularly dense texture.

storage Cake will keep for 1 day in an airtight container at room temperature.

hot chocolate prune cake

PREPARATION TIME 15 MINUTES • BAKING TIME 1 HOUR

Chocolate and prune are a texture and taste combination that was made in cakelovers' heaven. This cake has been prepared by being mixed in a food processor; some chocolate bits remain intact but they soften to melting point during baking.

1¼ cups (210g) seeded prunes
1¼ cups (310ml) boiling water
1 teaspoon bicarbonate of soda
60g butter, chopped
¾ cup (150g) firmly packed
   brown sugar
1 cup (150g) self-raising flour
2 eggs
100g dark chocolate,
   chopped coarsely

CHOCOLATE SAUCE
300ml cream
120g dark chocolate,
   chopped coarsely

1 Position oven shelves; preheat oven to moderate. Grease 20cm baba pan thoroughly.

2 Combine prunes and the water in bowl of food processor; add soda, place lid of processor in position; stand 5 minutes.

3 Add butter and sugar to processor, pulse until ingredients are just combined.

4 Add flour then eggs; pulse until ingredients are just combined.

5 Add chocolate; pulse until chocolate is just mixed into mixture (pieces of chocolate will still be visible). Pour mixture into prepared pan.

6 Bake cake in moderate oven about 1 hour. Stand cake 10 minutes then turn onto serving plate. Serve hot with chocolate sauce.

chocolate sauce Combine cream and chocolate in small saucepan; stir over low heat until chocolate is melted.

SERVES 8

per serving 32.5g fat; 2279kJ

TIPS This cake can also be made by the more conventional method: chop prunes, combine with the water and soda in a medium bowl, cover; stand 5 minutes. Using wooden spoon, stir in the finely chopped butter until melted then stir in sugar, lightly beaten eggs, flour and finely chopped chocolate. Follow baking directions at left.

• It is important the baba pan be well greased, because the cake mixture is both very wet and very sugary (two conditions making it likely to stick to the pan when baked).

• Freeze serving-size pieces of cake, individually sealed in freezer bags, to have a ready-to-serve dessert on hand. Thaw each piece on HIGH (100%) in a microwave oven for about 30 seconds; serve hot with cream and/or ice-cream. The chocolate sauce can also be reheated quickly in your microwave oven.

storage Cake will keep for up to 1 week in an airtight container at room temperature. If climate is humid, store cake in the refrigerator.

Cake can be frozen for up to 3 months.

Chopping chocolate coarsely

Adding eggs to prune mixture

Pouring mixture into prepared pan

TIPS Chopped seeded prunes or raisins can be substituted for dates.

• Polenta is the coarsely ground yellow cornmeal used for making cornmeal muffins and cornbread; it gives this cake a particularly dense texture.

• Brandy, rum, or your favourite liqueur can be substituted for Grand Marnier, and you can substitute the hazelnuts with any other variety of nut you like. Just be certain that you select a citrus fruit that complements the flavour of the liqueur and nuts you choose. For example, Cointreau, lemon rind and walnuts marry well, as do brandy, mandarin and pecans.

storage Cake will keep for up to 3 days in an airtight container at room temperature.

Rubbing skins off roasted hazelnuts

Coarsely chopping nuts

Adding nuts and undrained date mixture

Spreading ricotta filling over cake mixture

date, ricotta and polenta cake

PREPARATION TIME 30 MINUTES • BAKING TIME 1 HOUR 45 MINUTES

This is the perfect cake to serve at the end of an Italian meal, or with a cup of espresso when friends drop by in the late afternoon.

1 cup (160g) finely chopped seeded dates
1/3 cup (80ml) Grand Marnier
1/2 cup (60g) unroasted hazelnuts
2 cups (300g) self-raising flour
1 teaspoon baking powder
2/3 cup (110g) polenta
1 cup (220g) caster sugar
1 1/4 cups (250g) ricotta cheese
125g butter, melted
3/4 cup (180ml) water

RICOTTA FILLING

1 1/4 cups (250g) ricotta cheese
2 tablespoons Grand Marnier
2 tablespoons icing sugar mixture
1 tablespoon finely grated orange rind

1 Position oven shelves; preheat oven to moderately slow. Grease deep 22cm-round cake pan; line base and side with baking paper.

2 Combine dates and liqueur in small bowl; stand 15 minutes.

3 Meanwhile, roast nuts on oven tray in moderate oven about 10 minutes; wrap warm nuts in tea-towel, rub to remove skins. Chop nuts coarsely.

4 Combine flour, baking powder, polenta, sugar, cheese, butter and the water in large bowl; beat on low speed with electric mixer until just combined. Beat on medium speed until mixture changes to a lighter colour then, using wooden spoon, stir in nuts and undrained date mixture.

5 Spread half of the cake mixture into prepared pan; using metal spatula, spread ricotta filling over pan mixture then cover with remaining cake mixture.

6 Bake cake in moderately slow oven 45 minutes; cover tightly with foil, bake about 1 hour. Discard foil, stand cake in pan 10 minutes then turn onto wire rack; turn top-side up to cool.

ricotta filling Combine ingredients in medium bowl, stir with wooden spoon until smooth.

SERVES 16

per serving 12.7g fat; 1311kJ

mississippi mud cake

PREPARATION TIME 25 MINUTES • BAKING TIME 1 HOUR 30 MINUTES

This popular cake is a delectable alternative to fruit cake for weddings and other occasions. It is also wonderful after dinner with coffee, served warm or at room temperature with whipped cream and berries.

Coarsely chopping chocolate

250g butter, chopped coarsely
150g dark chocolate,
   chopped coarsely
2 cups (440g) caster sugar
1 cup (250ml) hot water
1/3 cup (80ml) coffee liqueur
1 tablespoon instant
   coffee powder
1 1/2 cups (225g) plain flour
1/4 cup (35g) self-raising flour
1/4 cup (25g) cocoa powder
2 eggs, beaten lightly

Adding chocolate to saucepan

1 Position oven shelves; preheat oven to moderately slow. Grease deep 20cm-round cake pan; line base and side with baking paper.

2 Combine butter, chocolate, sugar, the water, liqueur and coffee powder in medium saucepan. Using wooden spoon, stir over low heat until chocolate melts.

Whisking in sifted dry ingredients

3 Transfer mixture to large bowl; cool 15 minutes. Whisk in combined sifted flours and cocoa, then eggs. Pour mixture into prepared pan.

4 Bake cake in moderately slow oven about 1 1/2 hours. Stand cake 30 minutes then turn onto wire rack, turn cake top-side up to cool.

SERVES 16

per serving 16.7g fat; 1491kJ

Pouring cake mixture into prepared pan

TIPS Any coffee or chocolate-flavoured liqueur (Tia Maria, Kahlua or Crème de Cacao) can be used in this recipe.

• Cover cake loosely with foil about halfway through the baking time if it starts to overbrown.

• The melted chocolate mixture can be made in a large microwave-safe bowl on HIGH (100%) in the microwave oven for about 3 minutes, pausing to stir four times during cooking time.

storage Cake will keep for up to 1 week if placed in an airtight container in the refrigerator.

Cake can be frozen for up to 3 months.

rich truffle mud cake

PREPARATION TIME 15 MINUTES (plus refrigeration time)
BAKING TIME 1 HOUR

This very rich cake is perfect for the grand finale to a dinner party, and should be made a day ahead and served cold. The cake is almost like a huge truffle in texture; note that no flour is used.

6 eggs
¹/₂ cup (100g) firmly packed brown sugar
400g dark chocolate, melted
1 cup (250ml) thick cream (48% fat content)
¹/₃ cup (80ml) Cointreau

1 Position oven shelves; preheat oven to moderate. Grease deep 22cm-round cake pan; line base and side with baking paper.

2 Beat eggs and sugar in large bowl with electric mixer about 5 minutes or until thick and creamy. With motor operating, gradually beat in barely warm chocolate; beat until combined.

3 Using metal spoon, gently fold in combined cream and liqueur. Pour mixture into prepared pan.

4 Place pan in baking dish; pour enough boiling water into dish to come halfway up side of pan.

5 Bake cake in moderate oven 30 minutes. Cover loosely with foil; bake about 30 minutes. Discard foil; cool cake in pan.

6 Turn cake onto serving plate, cover; refrigerate overnight. Serve dusted with a little sifted cocoa, if desired.

SERVES 12

per serving 23.6g fat; 1523kJ

Adding melted chocolate to egg mixture

Folding in cream mixture

Pouring cake mixture into prepared pan

Pouring boiling water into baking dish

TIPS Melt chocolate in medium heatproof bowl placed over saucepan of hot water. Do not allow water in pan to touch bottom of the bowl containing chocolate. You can also stand the heatproof bowl in sink of hot water and stir the chocolate until it melts, or you can melt the chocolate in a microwave-safe bowl cooked on HIGH (100%) in the microwave oven, pausing to check the chocolate every 20 seconds.

• Any type of liqueur can be substituted for the citrus-flavoured Cointreau; you don't have to have a citrus flavour at all if you prefer some other taste such as rum or Frangelico, etc.

• The beauty of this cake is that it is completely finished a day ahead of party time.

• This cake is delicious served with fresh raspberries and fresh raspberry coulis.

storage Cake will keep for up to 4 days in an airtight container in the refrigerator.

rhubarb and pear custard cake

PREPARATION TIME 20 MINUTES • BAKING TIME 1 HOUR

A chocolate-free zone, this combination of fruit and custard is just as addictive. It's best served warm with cream.

Topping half of the mixture with half of the fruit

125g butter, softened
3/4 cup (165g) caster sugar
2 eggs
1 1/2 cups (225g) self-raising flour
1/2 cup (60g) almond meal
2 tablespoons custard powder
1/2 cup (125ml) milk
3 trimmed stalks (250g) rhubarb, sliced
1 large pear (330g), peeled, sliced thinly
1/2 cup (180g) apricot jam, warmed, strained

CUSTARD

2 tablespoons custard powder
2 tablespoons caster sugar
1 cup (250ml) milk
1 teaspoon vanilla essence
20g butter

Covering surface of custard with plastic wrap

1 Position oven shelves; preheat oven to moderate. Grease deep 22cm-round cake pan; line base and side with baking paper.

2 Beat butter and sugar in medium bowl with electric mixer until light and fluffy; add eggs, one at a time, beating well between additions. Using wooden spoon, stir in flour, almond meal, custard powder and milk.

3 Using metal spatula, spread half of the cake mixture into prepared pan, top with half of the rhubarb and pear.

Spreading custard over fruit

4 Spread custard over fruit; spread remaining cake mixture over custard, top with remaining rhubarb and pear.

5 Bake cake in moderate oven about 1 hour. Stand cake 5 minutes then turn onto wire rack; turn top-side up, brush top with warm jam. Cool.

custard Combine custard powder and sugar in small saucepan; using wooden spoon, gradually stir in milk. Stir over heat until mixture boils and thickens. Remove from heat, add vanilla and butter; stir until butter melts. Cover surface of custard completely with plastic wrap to prevent skin forming; cool to room temperature (do not refrigerate as mixture will not be spreadable).

SERVES 10

per serving 18.1g fat; 1742kJ

Topping cake mixture with remaining fruit

TIPS Large firm strawberries can be sliced lengthways and substituted for the rhubarb; apple or nashi can be substituted for the pear; or a combination of any of these fruits (including the rhubarb) can be used.

• Any jam can be substituted for apricot jam. Warm jam in the microwave oven for about 30 seconds on HIGH (100%); strain while warm.

• Any ground nuts can be substituted for almond meal; use a blender or processor to grind nuts finely.

storage Cake will keep for 1 day in an airtight container in the refrigerator.

family cakes

butterfly cakes

PREPARATION TIME 30 MINUTES • BAKING TIME 20 MINUTES

Butterfly cakes are made by removing a small circle of cake from the top of each patty cake, filling the cavity with your favourite jam and some cream, then topping the cream with the two halves of the circle to create "wings".

125g butter, softened
1 teaspoon vanilla essence
2/3 cup (150g) caster sugar
3 eggs
1 1/2 cups (225g) self-raising flour
1/4 cup (60ml) milk
1/2 cup (160g) jam
300ml thickened cream

1   Line two deep 12-hole patty pans with paper cases.

2   Combine butter, essence, sugar, eggs, flour and milk in small bowl of electric mixer; beat on low speed until ingredients are just combined. Increase speed to medium, beat about 3 minutes, or until mixture is smooth and changed to a paler colour.

3   Drop slightly rounded tablespoons of mixture into paper cases. Bake in moderate oven about 20 minutes. Turn cakes onto wire racks, turn top-side up to cool.

4   Using sharp pointed vegetable knife, cut circle from top of each cake; cut circle in half to make two "wings". Fill cavities with jam and whipped cream. Place wings in position on top of cakes; top with strawberry pieces and dust with a little sifted icing sugar, if desired.

MAKES 24

per serving 9.7g fat; 691kJ

Spooning mixture into paper cases

Cutting small circles from tops of cakes

Filling patty cakes with jam and cream

TIPS Use two paper patty cases in each patty pan hole for added stability for butterfly cakes.

storage Cakes are at their best made on day of serving. Once filled with cream, cakes should be refrigerated if made more than an hour ahead of time.

Unfilled cakes can be frozen for up to 1 month.

date and walnut rolls

PREPARATION TIME 15 MINUTES • BAKING TIME 50 MINUTES

An old-fashioned favourite, this classic nut roll, sliced and buttered, is perfect for afternoon tea. Nut roll tins are available from cookware shops and department stores.

60g butter
1 cup (250ml) boiling water
1 cup (180g) finely chopped seeded dried dates
1/2 teaspoon bicarbonate of soda
1 cup (200g) firmly packed brown sugar
2 cups (300g) self-raising flour
1/2 cup (65g) coarsely chopped walnuts
1 egg, beaten lightly

1 Position oven shelves; preheat oven to moderate. Grease two 8cm x 19cm nut roll tins, line bases with baking paper. Place tins upright on oven tray.

2 Combine butter and the water in medium saucepan; stir over low heat, using wooden spoon, until butter melts.

3 Transfer mixture to large bowl; stir in dates and soda, then sugar, flour, nuts and egg.

4 Spoon mixture into prepared tins; replace lids. Bake rolls, tins standing upright, in moderate oven about 50 minutes.

5 Stand rolls 5 minutes, remove all lids (top and bottom); shake tins gently to release nut rolls onto wire rack to cool.

SERVES 20

per serving 5.2g fat; 668kJ

Greasing nut roll tins

Mixing ingredients

Spooning mixture into tins

Removing nut rolls from tins

TIPS There are several different sizes and types of nut roll tins available, and it is important that you do not fill them with too much mixture. The nut rolls rise surprisingly high; both because the tin is so narrow and because the cooking method approximates that of steaming. As a loose guide, the tins should be filled just a little over halfway.

• Some nut roll tins open along the side; be certain these are closed properly before baking.

• Some lids have tiny holes in them to allow steam to escape; make sure these are not used on the bottom of the tins.

• Well-cleaned fruit juice cans can be used instead of the nut roll tins, and a double thickness of foil used as a substitute for lids. Again, remember to fill the tins just a little more than halfway.

storage Nut rolls will keep in an airtight container for up to 3 days.

Nut rolls can be frozen for up to 3 months.

ginger cake

PREPARATION TIME 15 MINUTES • BAKING TIME 1 HOUR 30 MINUTES

1¹/₂ cups (300g) firmly packed brown sugar
1¹/₂ cups (225g) plain flour
1¹/₂ cups (225g) self-raising flour
¹/₂ teaspoon bicarbonate of soda
1 tablespoon ground ginger
2 teaspoons ground cinnamon
1 teaspoon ground nutmeg
250g butter, softened
2 eggs
1 cup (250ml) buttermilk
¹/₂ cup (175g) golden syrup

LEMON FROSTING

60g butter, softened
2 teaspoons finely grated lemon rind
2 tablespoons lemon juice
2 cups (320g) icing sugar mixture

Cutting softened butter directly into bowl

Mixing ingredients until just combined

Spreading mixture into prepared pan

Adding juice and icing sugar to lemon frosting

1 Position oven shelves; preheat oven to moderately slow. Grease deep 23cm-square cake pan; line base with baking paper.

2 Sift dry ingredients into large bowl of electric mixer, add remaining ingredients. Beat mixture on low speed until ingredients are combined, then beat on medium speed until mixture is smooth and changed to a paler colour. Using metal spatula, spread mixture into prepared pan.

3 Bake cake in moderately slow oven about 1¹/₂ hours. Stand cake 10 minutes, turn onto wire rack, turn top-side up to cool. Spread cold cake with lemon frosting.

lemon frosting Using wooden spoon, beat butter and rind together in small bowl; gradually beat in juice and icing sugar.

SERVES 24

per serving 11.1g fat; 1194kJ

TIPS Cover cake loosely with foil about halfway through baking time if cake is overbrowning.

• If you like the stronger flavours of treacle or molasses, substitute either one for the golden syrup.

storage Frosted, this cake can be made 1 day ahead and kept in an airtight container; unfrosted, the cake will keep in an airtight container for up to 3 days.

Frosted or unfrosted, this cake can be frozen for up to 3 months.

Transferring flour mixture to bowl

Pressing base of cake into pan

Pouring topping mixture over base

cardamom-spiced cake

PREPARATION TIME 15 MINUTES • BAKING TIME 1 HOUR

An updated version of the Armenian nutmeg cake, this cake uses different spices and is more like a slice having a cake-like topping.

1 cup (150g) self-raising flour
1 cup (150g) plain flour
1¼ cups (250g) firmly packed brown sugar
1 teaspoon ground cinnamon
½ teaspoon ground nutmeg
½ teaspoon ground cardamom
¼ teaspoon ground cloves
125g butter, chopped
1 egg
1 teaspoon bicarbonate of soda
¾ cup (180ml) milk
½ cup (75g) shelled unsalted pistachios, chopped coarsely

1 Position oven shelves; preheat oven to moderate. Grease 20cm x 30cm lamington pan; line base and long sides of pan with baking paper.

2 Blend or process flours, sugar, spices and butter until ingredients resemble fine breadcrumbs. Transfer mixture to medium bowl.

3 Firmly press 1½ cups of the flour mixture evenly over base of prepared pan.

4 Use fork to combine egg, soda and milk in jug; add to remaining flour mixture with nuts, mix well with wooden spoon. Pour mixture over base in pan.

5 Bake cake in moderate oven about 1 hour. Stand cake 10 minutes then turn onto wire rack; turn cake top-side up to cool.

SERVES 15

per serving 10.5g fat; 981kJ

TIPS Any nuts, such as almonds, pecans, walnuts or hazelnuts, can be substituted for the pistachios.

• Butter should be chopped while still refrigerator-cold.

• Using a medium- to large-sized food processor or large blender will help make mixing of the butter through the dry ingredients quicker and easier; an alternative, however, is to finely chop or coarsely grate the cold butter then rub it through the dry ingredients with your fingertips.

storage Cake can be kept in an airtight container for up to 3 days.

Cake can be frozen for up to 1 month.

best-ever sponge cake

PREPARATION TIME 25 MINUTES • BAKING TIME 25 MINUTES

With just a little practice, anyone can become an expert sponge-maker.
Read our tips at right to help you on your way.

Fourth sifting of flour over egg mixture

Folding flour through egg mixture

Folding butter and water through egg mixture

4 eggs
3/4 cup (165g) caster sugar
1 cup (150g) self-raising flour
1 tablespoon cornflour
10g butter
1/3 cup (80ml) boiling water
1/3 cup (110g) lemon butter
3/4 cup (180ml) thickened cream
1 tablespoon icing sugar mixture

1 Position oven shelves; preheat oven to moderate. Grease two deep 20cm-round cake pans.

2 Beat eggs in large bowl with electric mixer until thick and foamy. Gradually add sugar, about a tablespoonful at a time, beating until sugar is dissolved between additions. Total beating time should be about 10 minutes.

3 Sift flour and cornflour together three times onto paper.

4 Sift flour mixture over egg mixture; using one hand like a rake, quickly and lightly fold and pull flour mixture through egg mixture, using the side of your hand as a scraper to make sure all the ingredients are combined.

5 Pour combined butter and the water down side of bowl; using one hand, fold through egg mixture. Pour mixture evenly into prepared pans, using metal spatula, spread mixture to edges of pans.

6 Bake sponges in moderate oven about 25 minutes. Immediately sponges are baked, turn onto wire racks covered with baking paper; turn top-side up to cool.

7 Place one sponge on serving plate, spread with lemon butter and whipped cream. Top with remaining cake, dust with sifted icing sugar.

SERVES 8

per serving 12.9g fat; 1322kJ

TIPS Beating the eggs and sugar well helps correctly aerate the mixture. Caster sugar dissolves the fastest; while crystal sugar can be used, it requires longer beating to be incorporated.

• It is important to create volume in the egg and sugar mixture; if you don't have a bowl like the one pictured, use a small bowl with deep sides and beat the mixture with either a hand-held or stand-mixer. You will get better results this way, even though you have to transfer the sponge mixture to a larger bowl to fold in the flour and water.

• If you don't like using your hand to mix ingredients, use a rubber or plastic spatula, or a large metal spoon.

• When the sponge is cooked, it will feel springy when touched gently with fingertips, and will have shrunk slightly away from the side of pan.

• Turn the sponge from cake pan as soon as it is baked, or heat from the pan will continue to cook it, giving it a too-crisp crust.

storage Sponge is best made on day of serving. Refrigerate if it is to be filled more than an hour ahead.

Unfilled sponge can be frozen for up to 1 month.

family chocolate cake

PREPARATION TIME 20 MINUTES • BAKING TIME 50 MINUTES

*One saucepan plus one large, heavy baking dish are practically all the equipment
needed to put together this easy, yummy chocolate cake.*

2 cups (500ml) water
3 cups (660g) caster sugar
250g butter, chopped
1/3 cup (35g) cocoa powder
1 teaspoon bicarbonate of soda
3 cups (450g) self-raising flour
4 eggs, beaten lightly

FUDGE FROSTING
90g butter
1/3 cup (80ml) water
1/2 cup (110g) caster sugar
**11/2 cups (240g) icing
  sugar mixture**
1/3 cup (35g) cocoa powder

1 Preheat oven to moderate. Grease deep 26.5cm x 33cm (14-cup/3.5-litre)
   baking dish; line base with baking paper.

2 Combine the water, sugar, butter and combined sifted cocoa and soda in
   medium saucepan; stir over heat, without boiling, until sugar dissolves.
   Bring to a boil then reduce heat; simmer, uncovered, 5 minutes. Transfer
   mixture to large bowl; cool to room temperature.

3 Add flour and egg to bowl; beat with electric mixer until mixture is smooth
   and changed to a paler colour. Pour mixture into prepared dish.

4 Bake cake in moderate oven about 50 minutes. Stand cake 10 minutes then
   turn onto wire rack; turn cake top-side up to cool.

5 Spread cold cake with fudge frosting.

   fudge frosting Combine butter, the water and caster sugar in small
   saucepan; stir over heat, without boiling, until sugar dissolves. Sift icing
   sugar and cocoa into small bowl then gradually stir in hot butter mixture.
   Cover; refrigerate about 20 minutes or until frosting thickens. Beat with
   wooden spoon until spreadable.

SERVES 20

per serving 15.8g fat; 1749kJ

Simmering water, sugar, butter, cocoa and soda

Pouring mixture into prepared pan

TIPS Choose a perfectly level-bottomed baking dish; one made from cast aluminium is the best choice, but almost any type will work.

• If the cake appears to be cooking too quickly in the corners of the pan, reduce oven temperature to moderately slow; this will increase cooking time by up to 15 minutes.

storage Cake will keep for up to 2 days in an airtight container at room temperature, or in the refrigerator for up to 4 days.

Frosted or unfrosted, this cake can be frozen for up to 1 month.

perfect honey roll

PREPARATION TIME 20 MINUTES • BAKING TIME 15 MINUTES

1 egg, separated
3 egg whites
2 tablespoons treacle
1/2 cup (175g) golden syrup
1/2 cup (75g) cornflour
1/3 cup (50g) self-raising flour
1 teaspoon ground ginger
1 teaspoon ground cinnamon
1/2 teaspoon ground nutmeg
1/4 teaspoon ground clove
2 tablespoons boiling water
1/2 teaspoon bicarbonate of soda
1/3 cup (30g) desiccated coconut

MOCK CREAM
1/2 cup (110g) caster sugar
1/2 teaspoon gelatine
1 tablespoon milk
1/3 cup (80ml) water
125g butter, softened
1/2 teaspoon vanilla essence

1 Position oven shelves; preheat oven to hot. Grease 25cm x 30cm swiss roll pan; line base and short sides with baking paper, bringing paper 5cm over edges. Grease the baking paper.

2 Beat the four egg whites in small bowl with electric mixer until soft peaks form; with motor operating, gradually add combined treacle and golden syrup in a thin stream.

3 Add egg yolk; beat until pale and thick. Transfer mixture to large bowl; using a metal spoon, fold in combined triple-sifted flours and spices, and combined water and soda. Pour mixture into prepared pan; gently spreading mixture evenly into corners.

4 Bake cake in hot oven about 15 minutes.

5 Meanwhile, place a piece of baking paper cut slightly larger than the cake on bench; sprinkle evenly with coconut. When cake is cooked, turn immediately onto paper, quickly peeling away the lining paper. Working rapidly, use serrated knife to carefully cut away crisp edges from all sides of cake.

6 Carefully roll cake loosely from one short side by lifting paper and using it to guide roll into shape; stand 10 seconds then unroll. Re-roll cake; cool to room temperature.

7 Gently unroll cake, spread with mock cream, carefully re-roll cake.

mock cream Combine sugar, gelatine, milk and water in small saucepan; stir over low heat, without boiling, until sugar and gelatine dissolve. Cool to room temperature. Beat butter and essence in small bowl with electric mixer until white and fluffy. With motor operating, gradually beat in sugar mixture until fluffy; this will take up to 15 minutes. Mock cream thickens on standing.

SERVES 8

per serving 16.3g fat; 1444kJ

TIPS While this is easy to make, it may take a bit of experimentation with your oven to determine the best temperature and to perfect the timing – two elements that are critical for the success of this sponge cake. Every oven is slightly different to another; be guided by your oven manufacturer's instructions. As a guide, the second shelf up from the oven floor is usually the best position for the cake pan and the temperature should be 200°C in a fan-forced oven.

• Gentle folding of the water and flour mixtures through the egg mixture is also important for success; heavy handling of the mixture equals a heavy sponge cake.

• Use whatever kitchen tool you feel most comfortable with to incorporate the ingredients. Some people prefer to use a large metal spoon, some their hand or a rubber or plastic spatula: it doesn't matter what you use, it's how you use it.

• Mock cream is a smooth mixture suitable for cream buns and other similar cakes but not thick enough to use for piping. It should not be refrigerated; because of the butter content, it will become rock hard. Cake can be filled up to 2 hours before required.

storage Cake is best made on the day it is served.

Trimming edges of sponge

Rolling sponge in baking paper

Spreading sponge with mock cream

TIPS This cake can also be baked in a deep 20cm-round cake pan that has its base lined with baking paper. Bake in moderate oven for about 1 hour.

• These icings are known as glacé icings, and are sometimes also called warm icings. The most important part in making them successfully is taking care not to overheat the mixture as it's being stirred; since sugar crystallises when overheated, your icing with be overly thick and gritty textured. One tried-and-true way is to stand the bowl containing the paste in a sink or dish of hot water, stirring it until it becomes smooth, glossy and barely warm, then pouring it over the cake immediately before it has the chance to set. A glass, china or metal bowl can be used but plastic is not a good conductor of heat.

storage Cake will keep in an airtight container for up to 3 days.

Un-iced cake can be frozen for up to 3 months.

Stirring icing to a thick paste

Pouring peppermint icing over cake

Pouring chocolate icing over peppermint icing

chocolate peppermint cake

PREPARATION TIME 30 MINUTES • BAKING TIME 1 HOUR

The popular combination of chocolate and peppermint makes this an extremely more-ish cake.

185g butter, softened
1 teaspoon vanilla essence
1 cup (220g) caster sugar
3 eggs
2/3 cup (160ml) milk
2 cups (300g) self-raising flour
5 tablespoons cocoa powder

PEPPERMINT ICING
1 1/2 cups (240g) icing
  sugar mixture
1 teaspoon butter
2 tablespoons milk,
  approximately
peppermint essence

CHOCOLATE ICING
1 1/2 cups (240g) icing
  sugar mixture
2 tablespoons cocoa powder
1 teaspoon butter
2 tablespoons water,
  approximately

1 Position oven shelves; preheat oven to moderate. Grease 20cm baba pan thoroughly.

2 Beat butter, essence and sugar in small bowl with electric mixer until light and fluffy; add eggs, one at a time, beat until combined.

3 Transfer mixture to large bowl; using wooden spoon, stir in milk and combined sifted flour and cocoa in two batches. Spoon mixture into prepared pan.

4 Bake cake in moderate oven about 1 hour. Stand cake in pan 5 minutes then turn onto wire rack to cool.

5 Pour peppermint icing over cold cake; allow to set at room temperature. Pour chocolate icing over peppermint icing; allow to set at room temperature.

peppermint icing Place icing sugar in small heatproof bowl; using wooden spoon, stir in butter and enough milk to make a firm paste. Flavour with a few drops of essence. Stand bowl over small saucepan of simmering water, stirring until icing is of a spreading consistency (do not overheat).

chocolate icing Sift icing sugar and cocoa into small heatproof bowl; using wooden spoon, stir in butter and enough of the water to make a firm paste. Stand bowl over small saucepan of simmering water, stirring until icing is of a spreading consistency (do not overheat).

SERVES 12

per serving 16.4g fat; 1982kJ

apple streusel cake

PREPARATION TIME 20 MINUTES • BAKING TIME 50 MINUTES

This cake, completely finished after baking since it has its own topping, is simply delicious. We used Granny Smith apples in our version.

3 medium apples (450g)
1 tablespoon caster sugar
1/4 cup (60ml) water
185g butter, softened
3/4 cup (165g) caster sugar, extra
2 eggs
21/4 cups (335g) self-raising flour
3/4 cup (180ml) milk

CINNAMON STREUSEL TOPPING
3/4 cup (110g) plain flour
3 teaspoons ground cinnamon
60g butter, chopped
1/3 cup (75g) firmly packed brown sugar
2 teaspoons water, approximately

Coring the peeled apple quarters

Layering apple over cake mixture

Coarsely grating streusel topping mixture

Sprinkling streusel topping over cake mixture

1 Position oven shelves; preheat oven to moderate. Grease deep 23cm-square cake pan; line base with baking paper.

2 Peel, core and quarter apples; slice thinly. Combine apple, sugar and the water in medium saucepan; bring to a boil. Reduce heat; simmer, covered, about 10 minutes or until apple is tender, drain well.

3 Meanwhile, beat butter and extra sugar in small bowl with electric mixer until light and fluffy. Add eggs, one at a time, beating well between additions. Transfer mixture to large bowl; using wooden spoon, stir in flour and milk, in two batches.

4 Spread two-thirds of the mixture evenly over base of prepared pan, top evenly with apple, then spread with remaining mixture. Sprinkle evenly with cinnamon streusel topping.

5 Bake cake in moderate oven about 50 minutes. Stand cake 5 minutes then turn onto wire rack; turn cake top-side up to cool.

cinnamon streusel topping Combine flour and cinnamon in small bowl; rub in butter with fingertips, add sugar. Using one hand, mix in enough of the water to make mixture come together in a ball, cover with plastic wrap; freeze 30 minutes. Coarsely grate topping mixture before sprinkling on unbaked cake.

SERVES 12

per serving 18.7g fat; 1644kJ

TIPS Canned pie apple can be used instead of stewed fresh apples. If using canned apple, omit apples, sugar and water from ingredient list at left.

• Any other stewed or canned fruit can be substituted for apple but it is important that whatever fruit you use is as dry as possible; excess moisture will make the cake doughy. Fruit which has been canned in water or syrup should be drained then placed on absorbent paper for at least 10 minutes.

• Cake can also be baked in a 20cm x 30cm lamington pan, its base lined with baking paper. Bake cake in moderate oven about 50 minutes.

storage Cake will keep for up to 2 days in an airtight container at room temperature, or in the refrigerator for up to 3 days.

marble cake

PREPARATION TIME 30 MINUTES • BAKING TIME 1 HOUR

Very popular with children, this cake's traditional colours are chocolate brown, pink and white, but you can use any food colouring you like to tint the mixture. Make the colours fairly strong for maximum impact: colour can lessen in intensity during baking, and kids love this cake when it's bright.

Tinting a third of cake mixture pink

Flavouring a third of cake mixture chocolate

Spooning alternate colours of mixture into pan

Marbling mixture with skewer

250g butter, softened
1 teaspoon vanilla essence
1¼ cups (275g) caster sugar
3 eggs
2¼ cups (335g)
   self-raising flour
¾ cup (180ml) milk
pink food colouring
2 tablespoons cocoa powder
1 tablespoon milk, extra

PINK BUTTER FROSTING
90g butter
1 cup (160g) icing sugar mixture
1 tablespoon milk
pink food colouring

1 Position oven shelves; preheat oven to moderate. Grease deep 22cm-round cake pan; line base with baking paper.

2 Beat butter, essence and sugar in medium bowl with electric mixer until light and fluffy. Add eggs, one at a time, beating until combined. Using wooden spoon, stir in flour and milk, in two batches.

3 Divide mixture evenly among three bowls; tint mixture in one bowl pink by stirring through a few drops of colouring with a wooden spoon.

4 Using a teaspoon, blend sifted cocoa with extra milk in cup; stir into the second bowl of mixture.

5 Drop alternate spoonfuls of the three coloured mixtures into prepared pan.

6 Pull a skewer backwards and forwards through cake mixture several times for a marbled effect; smooth surface with metal spatula.

7 Bake cake in moderate oven about 1 hour. Stand cake 5 minutes then turn onto wire rack; turn cake top-side up to cool.

pink butter frosting Beat butter in small bowl with electric mixer until light and fluffy; beat in icing sugar and milk, in two batches. Using wooden spoon, beat in a few drops of colouring to tint frosting pink.

SERVES 12

per serving 25.8g fat; 1988kJ

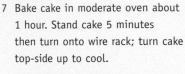

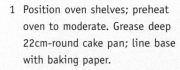

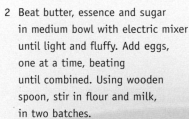

TIPS There are many types of food colourings available – pastes, gels, powders and liquids. Since they all vary greatly in strength, start tinting by using only a drop or a tiny amount, then increase the amount until you get the strength of colour you desire.

storage Cake will keep for up to 2 days in an airtight container at room temperature, or in the refrigerator for up to 4 days.

Frosted or unfrosted, this cake can be frozen for up to 1 month.

TIPS It is very important to thoroughly drain the pineapple, or else the cake will be doughy and heavy.

• Toasting macadamias brings out the flavour. There are two ways to toast them: spread macadamias onto an oven tray, toast nuts in moderate oven for 5 to 10 minutes, or until they are golden brown (stir nuts once during toasting for even browning); alternatively, place macadamias in heavy-base frying pan, stir nuts constantly over medium-to-high heat until they are evenly browned.

• Cake can also be baked in two 8cm x 25cm bar cake pans, the bases of which have been lined with baking paper. Bake cakes in moderate oven about 25 minutes.

storage This cake will keep for 1 day in an airtight container, or 2 days in the refrigerator.

pineapple macadamia loaf

PREPARATION TIME 15 MINUTES • BAKING TIME 50 MINUTES

This is a very quick and easy cake to make that only involves hand-mixing in one bowl. The recipe contains no butter, but the finished cake is delicious served with lashings of butter.

450g can crushed pineapple
1 egg
1 cup (150g) macadamias,
   toasted, chopped finely
1 cup (150g) self-raising flour
¹/₂ cup (110g) caster sugar
1 cup (90g) desiccated coconut
¹/₂ cup (125ml) milk

Toasted macadamia nuts

1 Position oven shelves; preheat oven to moderate. Grease 14cm x 21cm loaf pan, line base with baking paper.

2 Drain pineapple, pressing as much syrup as possible from the pineapple; discard syrup.

Pressing syrup from pineapple

3 Place pineapple in large bowl, add egg; stir ingredients together with wooden spoon. Stir in remaining ingredients; mix well. Spread mixture into prepared pan.

4 Bake cake in moderate oven about 50 minutes.

5 Stand cake 10 minutes, turn onto wire rack, then turn top-side up to cool.

Stirring all ingredients together

SERVES 20

per serving 9.1g fat; 602kJ

Spreading mixture into prepared pan

glossary

clockwise from front left: choc bits, chocolate melts and cooking chocolate

almond

FLAKED paper-thin slices.

KERNELS natural nut with brown skin intact.

MEAL also known as ground almonds; nuts are powdered to a flour-like texture, for use in baking or as a thickening agent.

SLIVERED small lengthways-cut pieces.

baking powder raising agent consisting mainly of two parts cream of tartar to one part bicarbonate of soda.

beetroot also known as red beets or simply beets; firm, round root vegetable which can be eaten raw, grated in salads, boiled or microwaved then mashed, or roasted.

bicarbonate of soda also known as baking soda.

butter use salted or unsalted ("sweet") butter; 125g is equal to one stick of butter.

buttermilk sold alongside all fresh milk products in supermarkets. A good lower-fat substitute for dairy products such as cream or sour cream; good in baking and in salad dressings.

canola oil a mono-unsaturated oil made from rapeseed which is simultaneously low in saturated fats and high in Omega-3 fatty acids; good used in cooking or in salad dressing.

chocolate

CHOC BITS also known as chocolate chips and chocolate morsels; available in milk, white and dark chocolate. These hold their shape in baking and are ideal as a cake decoration.

DARK COOKING we used premium-quality dark cooking chocolate rather than compound.

MELTS discs made of milk, white or dark chocolate compound; good for melting and moulding.

cocoa powder also known as cocoa; unsweetened, dried, roasted then ground cocoa beans.

coconut

DESICCATED unsweetened, concentrated, dried shredded coconut.

FLAKED dried, flaked coconut flesh.

SHREDDED thin strips of dried coconut flesh.

coffee-flavoured liqueur Tia Maria, Kahlua or any generic brand.

colourings many types are available from cake decorating suppliers, craft shops and some supermarkets; all are concentrated. Use a minute amount of any type of colouring first to determine its strength.

LIQUID the strength varies depending on the quality; useful for colouring most types of icings where pastel colours are needed. Large amounts of liquid colourings will dilute or break down most icings.

POWDERED these are edible and are used when primary colours or black are needed.

CONCENTRATED PASTES these are a little more expensive but are the easiest to use; are suitable for both pastel and stronger colours.

cointreau a citrus-flavoured, clear, French liqueur.

cornflour also known as cornstarch; used as a thickening agent in cooking.

corn syrup a thick sweet syrup made by processing cornstarch; available in light (vanilla flavoured) or dark (caramel flavoured) varieties. Used as an ingredient in frostings and jam- and jelly-making, and as a topping for ice-cream and pancakes.

cream

SOUR (minimum fat content 35%) a thick, commercially cultured soured cream.

THICK (minimum fat content 48%) a rich, pure cream not suitable for whipping.

THICKENED (minimum fat content 35%) a whipping cream containing a thickener.

custard powder packaged powdered mixture of starch (wheat or corn), artificial flavouring and colouring. Sometimes sold as vanilla pudding mixture.

dried currants tiny, almost-black raisins so-named after a grape variety that originated in Corinth, Greece.

essence also known as extract; a flavouring extracted from various plants by distillation.

flour

PLAIN an all-purpose flour, made from wheat.

SELF-RAISING all-purpose flour sifted with baking powder in the proportion of 1 cup flour to 2 teaspoons baking powder.

WHOLEMEAL also known as all-purpose wholemeal flour; has no baking powder added.

frangelico hazelnut-flavoured liqueur.

fruit mince also known as mince meat.

gelatine (gelatin) we used powdered gelatine as a setting agent. It is also available in sheets called leaf gelatine.

glacé cherries also known as candied cherries; cherries cooked in heavy sugar syrup then dried.

golden syrup a by-product of refined sugarcane; pure maple syrup or honey can be substituted.

grand marnier a brandy-based, orange-flavoured liqueur.

hazelnut meal also known as ground hazelnuts; the nut is roasted then powdered to a flour-like texture for use in baking.

jam also known as preserves or conserve.

kirsch a clear brandy made from morello cherries and their seeds.

lemon butter also known as lemon curd, lemon cheese or lemon spread; a creamed mixture made from lemon juice and/or rind, egg yolks, butter and sugar, in varying proportions.

maple-flavoured syrup made from sugar cane rather than maple-tree sap; used in cooking or as a topping but cannot be considered an exact substitute for pure maple syrup.

marsala a sweet fortified wine originally from Sicily.

marzipan meal made from ground apricot kernels; a less-expensive substitute for almond meal.

mascarpone a fresh, unripened, thick, triple-cream cheese with a delicately sweet, slightly acidic flavour.

mixed fruit also known as mixed dried fruit; commonly a combination of sultanas, raisins, currants, mixed peel and cherries.

mixed peel also known as candied citrus peel.

mixed spice a blend of ground spices usually consisting of cinnamon, allspice and nutmeg.

polenta a flour-like cereal made of ground corn (maize); similar to cornmeal but finer and paler.

rhubarb a vegetable of which only the firm, reddish stems are edible; the toxic leaves are always discarded.

ricotta sweet, moist, fresh curd cheese having a low fat content.

rind also known as zest; the outer layer of all citrus fruits.

sugar we used coarse, granulated table sugar, also known as crystal sugar, unless otherwise specified.

BLACK less refined than brown sugar and containing more molasses; mostly used in making Christmas cakes, this is available from health food stores.

BROWN a soft, fine granulated sugar containing molasses to give its characteristic colour.

CASTER also known as superfine or finely granulated table sugar.

DEMERARA small-grained, golden-coloured crystal sugar.

ICING SUGAR MIXTURE also known as confectioners' sugar or powdered sugar; crushed granulated sugar with added cornflour (about 3%).

PURE ICING also known as confectioners' sugar but without the addition of cornflour.

sultanas also known as golden raisins; dried, seedless, white grapes.

treacle thick, dark syrup not unlike molasses; a by-product of refined sugar.

vanilla essence distilled from the seeds of the vanilla pod; imitation vanilla extract is not a satisfactory substitute.

vegetable oil any of a number of oils sourced from plants rather than animal fats.

index

ARE YOU MISSING SOME OF THE WORLD'S FAVOURITE COOKBOOKS?

The Australian Women's Weekly Cookbooks are available from bookshops, cookshops, supermarkets and other stores all over the world. You can also buy direct from the publisher, using the order form below.

TITLE	RRP	QTY	TITLE	RRP	QTY
Asian Meals in Minutes	£6.99		Great Lamb Cookbook	£6.99	
Babies & Toddlers Good Food	£6.99		Greek Cooking Class	£6.99	
Barbecue Meals In Minutes	£6.99		Healthy Heart Cookbook	£6.99	
Basic Cooking Class	£6.99		Indian Cooking Class	£6.99	
Beginners Cooking Class	£6.99		Japanese Cooking Class	£6.99	
Beginners Simple Meals	£6.99		Kids' Birthday Cakes	£6.99	
Beginners Thai	£6.99		Kids Cooking	£6.99	
Best Food	£6.99		Lean Food	£6.99	
Best Food Desserts	£6.99		Low-carb, Low-fat	£6.99	
Best Food Fast	£6.99		Low-fat Feasts	£6.99	
Best Food Mains	£6.99		Low-fat Food For Life	£6.99	
Cakes, Biscuits & Slices	£6.99		Low-fat Meals in Minutes	£6.99	
Cakes Cooking Class	£6.99		Main Course Salads	£6.99	
Caribbean Cooking	£6.99		Middle Eastern Cooking Class	£6.99	
Casseroles	£6.99		Midweek Meals in Minutes	£6.99	
Chicken	£6.99		Muffins, Scones & Breads	£6.99	
Chicken Meals in Minutes	£6.99		New Casseroles	£6.99	
Chinese Cooking Class	£6.99		New Classics	£6.99	
Christmas Cooking	£6.99		New Finger Food	£6.99	
Chocolate	£6.99		Party Food and Drink	£6.99	
Cocktails	£6.99		Pasta Meals in Minutes	£6.99	
Cooking for Friends	£6.99		Potatoes	£6.99	
Creative Cooking on a Budget	£6.99		Salads: Simple, Fast & Fresh	£6.99	
Detox	£6.99		Saucery	£6.99	
Dinner Beef	£6.99		Sauces, Salsas & Dressings	£6.99	
Dinner Lamb	£6.99		Sensational Stir-Fries	£6.99	
Dinner Seafood	£6.99		Short-order Cook	£6.99	
Easy Australian Style	£6.99		Slim	£6.99	
Easy Curry	£6.99		Sweet Old-fashioned Favourites	£6.99	
Easy Spanish-style Cookery	£6.99		Thai Cooking Class	£6.99	
Essential Soup	£6.99		Vegetarian Meals in Minutes	£6.99	
Freezer, Meals from the	£6.99		Vegie Food	£6.99	
French Food, New	£6.99		Weekend Cook	£6.99	
Fresh Food for Babies & Toddlers	£6.99		Wicked Sweet Indulgences	£6.99	
Get Real, Make a Meal	£6.99		Wok Meals in Minutes	£6.99	
Good Food Fast	£6.99		TOTAL COST:	£	

Mr/Mrs/Ms _____

Address _____

_____ Postcode _____

Day time phone _____ Email* (optional) _____

I enclose my cheque/money order for £ _____

or please charge £ _____

to my: ☐ Access ☐ Mastercard ☐ Visa ☐ Diners Club

PLEASE NOTE: WE DO NOT ACCEPT SWITCH OR ELECTRON CARDS

Card number ☐☐☐☐☐☐☐☐☐☐☐☐☐☐☐☐

Expiry date _____ 3 digit security code (found on reverse of card) _____

Cardholder's name_____ Signature _____

To order: Mail or fax – photocopy or complete the order form above, and send your credit card details or cheque payable to: Australian Consolidated Press (UK), Moulton Park Business Centre, Red House Road, Moulton Park, Northampton NN3 6AQ, phone (+44) (0) 1604 497531 fax (+44) (0) 1604 497533, e-mail books@acpmedia.co.uk or order online at www.acpuk.com

Non-UK residents: We accept the credit cards listed on the coupon, or cheques, drafts or International Money Orders payable in sterling and drawn on a UK bank. Credit card charges are at the exchange rate current at the time of payment.

Postage and packing UK: Add £1.00 per order plus 50p per book.

Postage and packing overseas: Add £2.00 per order plus £1.00 per book.

All pricing current at time of going to press and subject to change/availability.
Offer ends 31.12.2007

* By including your email address, you consent to receipt of any email regarding this magazine, and other emails which inform you of ACP's other publications, products, services and events, and to promote third party goods and services you may be interested in.